MAKE

YOUR

MEMORY

MAKE YOUR MEMORY

THE MODERN CRAFTER'S GUIDE TO BEAUTIFUL

SCRAPBOOK LAYOUTS, CARDS, AND MINI ALBUMS

PAIGE EVANS

BETTER DAY BOOKS®

HAPPY · CREATIVE · CURATED

Easy SVG Downloads!

Download all the ready-to-use digital cut files for the designs used in the projects in this book at the following link. Every design is provided in SVG, STUDIO3, and PDF format. If you don't own an electronic cutting machine, don't worry—you can just print and cut out the PDF designs at home on your printer!

www.betterdaybooks.com/make-your-memory-svg-download

Make Your Memory © 2023 by Paige Evans and Better Day Books, Inc.

Publisher: Peg Couch
Cover Designer: Paige Evans and Ashlee Wadeson
Book Designer: Llara Pazdan
Editor: Colleen Dorsey
Photo Stylist (finished projects): Lori Wenger
Photographer (finished projects): Jason Masters
Photographer (step-by-step and workspace): Paige Evans

The following images are credited to Freepik.com and their respective creators: dedication box (page 5): macrovector; photo corners (page 16 and similar): a-r-t-u-r; scrapbook patterns (pages 4–5, 12–13, 38–39, 112–113, 136–137, 160, 161–176, and similar): freepik. The following image is credited to Flaticon.com and its respective creator: SVG icon (page 4): Maan Icons

Library of Congress Control Number: 2022947656

ISBN: 978-0-7643-6658-1
Printed in China
First printing

Copublished by Better Day Books, Inc., and Schiffer Publishing, Ltd.

Better Day Books
P.O. Box 21462
York, PA 17402
Phone: 717-487-5523
Email: hello@betterdaybooks.com
www.betterdaybooks.com
@better_day_books

Schiffer Publishing
4880 Lower Valley Road
Atglen, PA 19310
Phone: 610-593-1777
Fax: 610-593-2002
Email: info@schifferbooks.com
www.schifferbooks.com

This title is available for promotional or commercial use, including special editions. Contact info@schifferbooks.com for more information.

Dedication

To my mom: thanks for making me get a job that has led to all of this. To my husband, Chris, my biggest supporter and helper. And to Fox and Jane, the subjects of almost all of my scrapbook layouts.

CONTENTS

WELCOME!

If you have always wanted to amp up your creativity when it comes to keeping memories, then I wrote this book for you. You'll learn how to use treasured family photos and beautiful craft supplies to make nine modern scrapbook layouts, five greeting cards for a variety of occasions, and three stunning mini albums.

My passion for scrapbooking runs deep. I often spend hours on single pages—they are truly labors of love for me—and I have many signature scrapbook collections with American Crafts. Now, I'm excited to share my years of experience with you in this comprehensive guide. I'll teach you the best tips, tricks, and techniques to use for your creations, from the right glue for every project, to simple creases and folds for adding dimension, to how to design with symmetry and balance even in busy compositions. Plus, there are several sheets of scrapbook paper bound right into the back of this book, perforated for easy tear-out!

I hope to inspire you to try new things and to truly dedicate yourself to making your memories. So, what are you waiting for? Let's get scrapping!

Paige Taylor Evans

MEET THE AUTHOR

How did you first get started in scrapbooking?

I was first introduced at a church activity when I was 10 years old at our neighbor's house across the street. Then, when I was 16 years old, my parents told me I needed to get a job to pay for gas for my car, so I started working at a local scrapbook store (or LSS, as they're called in scrapbook circles). The rest, as they say, is history!

How did you develop your art style?

When I first started scrapbooking in the early 2000s, grunge and distressing were all the rage, so I was all aboard that train! The day I started working as an in-house scrapbooker for the company American Crafts, my style instantly changed to light and bright, which really connected with my soul.

When did you first start teaching scrapbooking?

At age 17 as an employee at Yesterday's Scrapbooking & Stuff, the owners saw the creations I was making and offered me the chance to teach classes. I was so grateful for the opportunity; I actually still have a bag full of the cards I taught how to make!

What do you love most about scrapbooking?

I love the creation process. Making something from nothing with my hands brings me so much satisfaction and joy!

You wear a lot of hats—what are they, and what's your day-to-day like?

I collaborate with American Crafts to design signature scrapbooking collections. I design digital cut files to sell in my shop and on the Silhouette, Inc., website. I am the creative editor for *Scrapbook & Cards Today* magazine. I also teach online and in-person classes whenever and wherever I can! Aside from work (though I wouldn't call it work—I love it too much!), I'm a wife and mom. To be honest, I will forever be working on balancing all my roles.

Besides scrapbooking, what are your passions?

I love my cats—does that count? Call me crazy cat lady! In all seriousness, I love to travel, find new places to eat, go to the movies, and watch/listen to true crime all day every day as I'm working.

What do you hope people take away from this book?

I hope people are excited to try scrapbooking and cardmaking if they haven't already, and then re-create these same projects and share them so I can see! I love seeing how people take ideas and translate them into their own projects.

What is your advice to a beginner?

Don't overthink it, and embrace imperfections. I'll never notice if something is crooked or a bit torn, and others won't either. If you're happy with your creations, that's what really matters!

Is there anything else you'd like to share?

If at first you don't succeed, don't give up—try again later, after you've made adjustments or worked on it to improve. My idea for a scrapbook collection was denied at first, so I worked really hard for the next few years to say yes to opportunities and guest design spots, and then I felt more confident to pitch a scrapbook collection again. You never know until you ask! The worst someone can say is no, but what if they say yes?

Dreams do come true.

ABOUT PAIGE

Paige Evans is a prolific paper artist and craft designer who is well known for her intricate scrapbook layouts, beautiful handmade cards, and layered photo albums. She has 15 signature scrapbook collections with American Crafts (with more on the way), regularly designs cut files for Silhouette, Inc., and is the creative editor for *Scrapbook & Cards Today* magazine. A passionate and in-demand instructor, Paige has more than 30 scrapbooking and mini-album workshops available online and loves teaching in-person workshops whenever she can. Paige resides in Littleton, Colorado, with her husband, two children, and two curious kittens who love to hang out in her craft studio! To learn more, please visit *www.paigetaylorevans.com* and @paigetaylorevans on Instagram.

GETTING STARTED

What do you need to get started in scrapbooking? What kind of paper can you use? How do you choose photos? What kind of embellishments will work? How can you effectively design a new page? And how can you organize your growing stash of tools and supplies? I'll explain all of this in detail in this first chapter!

PAPER

Ask me what my favorite scrapbook supply is, and without a doubt I will immediately say patterned paper. All the colors, patterns, and potential—paper is my jam!

In each of my collections with American Crafts, there are 24 double-sided patterned papers that coordinate perfectly together and that are almost always the foundation for my pages and projects. Patterned papers come in many different themes to match special occasions, from baby and birthdays, to pets and vacations, and everything between!

Cardstock is also an essential. I personally love to use cardstock for the foundation of my pages, projects, and cut files. Cardstock comes in many different styles and thicknesses. My favorite is textured cardstock with a weight of 80 lbs., and I tend to use white as well as bright rainbow colors that coordinate with my chosen patterned papers. There is also smooth cardstock,

cardstock with different embossed patterns and weaves, glitter cardstock, shiny cardstock, and many more options! Another option to consider incorporating is kraft cardstock, which comes in different shades and is a great neutral.

In addition to patterned papers and cardstock, two other types of papers in scrapbooking are vellum and transparencies. Vellum is popular for making shaker pockets (sealed areas containing loose items) and comes in many colors, though the most popular type is colorless. Transparencies come in clear as well as patterned varieties and are also used for shakers and for fun mix-and-match projects with a bunch of different media. Patterned transparencies are great for mini album covers—you'll see an example of one such application in one of the featured projects in this book!

From smooth and textured cardstock, to papers in so many colors and patterns, to special transparencies, endless paper options are sure to stoke your creativity.

TOOLS AND SUPPLIES

Basic tools that you'll need in scrapbooking and will reach for time and time again include a 12" paper trimmer, scissors, and various adhesives. Other tools that aren't essential but that can be game changers include punches, an electronic cutting machine, a sewing machine, and hand-stitching supplies. And, of course, there are lots of extra tools on the market that aren't essential but are fun to have and try!

There are a few other basic tools that I recommend always keeping within arm's reach as you're crafting: a standard hole punch, a pencil and eraser, journaling pens to write your stories, a bone folder for making crisp folds and creases, a craft knife, and a spatula for scraping off sticky cutting mats for electronic cutting machines.

Trimmer and Scoring Board

I've used my 12" trimmer (mine is from Fiskars) for more than 20 years. It's loved and worn and perfect. When choosing a trimmer, look for one that is compact, lightweight, and easy to use; one that has a pullout ruler for exact measuring; one for which the replacement blades are easy to find online and in craft stores; and, most importantly, one that cuts paper and photos clean and straight. There are many paper trimmers on the market; read reviews and ask your friends their favorites before committing to one.

I also recommend having a scoring board and tool on hand. I use mine often to make score lines for folding papers that go into mini albums. Score lines make clean creases.

Scissors

A good collection of scissors is something you'll reach for time and again. My collection includes standard, fine-tipped, fringe, thread trimming, and deco scissors. The first three are the hard workers that I personally use all the time, and the other two are more specialized. No matter your style, you'll definitely need the first two.

- **Standard scissors** are the go-to when cutting a stack of papers or more than one paper at a time. They're also ideal for opening packages.
- My **fine-tipped scissors** get the most use. In scrapbooking, the term for cutting out individual images, icons, and designs from a patterned paper is called fussy-cutting.

You either love it or you hate it—and I love it. Fine-tipped scissors with a sharp edge and smaller blades get the job done nicely, making it easiest for you to cut as close to the image as possible.

- **Fringe scissors**, or herb-cutting scissors, have multiple blades combined into a single set of scissors. Fringes are a fun and textured item for dressing up your pages.
- A tiny pair of scissors or **embroidery scissors** are ideal for trimming thread.
- Last, I do have a little bucket with **deco scissors**! You know the ones I'm talking about: ones that cut pinked, wavy, scalloped, and other kinds of edges! I tend to use my deco scissors not to cut out photos, but instead to create fun and interesting paper strips and borders for embellishing.

Punches

I. Love. Punches. As you'll see on many of the projects featured in this book, I use punches often. Why? For several reasons. First, as I mentioned before, patterned paper is my favorite scrapbook supply. The more papers I can use on a layout, the better! Punches make it really easy to add a bunch of patterned papers quickly. Second, my design aesthetic revolves, more often than not, around the design concept of repetition. I take one idea and repeat it (usually with patterned paper) to create a fun and colorful page. Punches help with the repetition part of that concept. I have an entire chest of drawers filled with different punches. From borders and basic shapes like stars, hearts, butterflies, squares, flowers, and hexagons, to more-themed shapes such as snowflakes, cupcakes, clouds, and bows, I have and will continue to hoard and use punches on my projects!

Adhesives

Adhesives you'll probably want to have on hand include an adhesive dispenser, rolls of super-sticky double-sided tape in various widths (from $1/8$" to 1"), liquid adhesive, glue dots, foam squares, spray adhesive, hot glue, and (sparingly) superglue.

- An **adhesive dispenser** is the quickest and easiest way to attach this to that. However, after scrapbooking for more than 20 years, I have found that even dispensers that claim to be "permanent" have not stood the test of time, and I've spent many hours putting older pages back together. Now I only use an adhesive dispenser if I know I'm going to go back and secure whatever I'm attaching with a more permanent solution, such as liquid glue or a sewing machine.

- **Super-sticky double-sided tape** is great for making things stick for good. The rolls of varying widths mean you can attach itty bitty edges that are only $1/8$", cover a large surface area quickly with 1" tape, and achieve everything in between. However, I don't recommend stitching through this type of adhesive, as it gums up the needle quickly, so plan ahead.

- **Liquid adhesive** is my favorite. Sometimes I like to say, "Adhesive has one job: to stick!" Liquid adhesive gets the job done,

and it lasts. I use liquid glue to attach almost everything in place, whether I'm making scrapbook layouts, cards, or mini albums. Get a bottle with a tiny nozzle that dispenses only a little glue at a time—that way, you can get the glue exactly where you need it quickly, and it will dry fast.

- **Glue dots** allow you to attach materials that the other types of glue won't adhere to well, including plastic, such as buttons, sequins, and acrylic pieces, and metal, such as charms and small magnets. Glue dots also attach well to thread, fabric, and other fibrous materials.

- **Foam squares** are great for adding dimension and helping things literally pop off the page or background. I used them for the words on the cover of this book! Look for ones that aren't too thick, because the thicker the dots, the fewer pages you'll be able to fit into a single scrapbook. I like thinner foam squares that add depth and shadows but still let me squeeze lots of layouts into an album.

- **Spray adhesive** is a great solution for attaching a bunch of small shapes onto the back of a cut file. Instead of adding glue around each segment of a shape or a design, spray the entire back side and then place the little inner pieces quickly to back the cut file.

- **Hot glue** is mostly reserved for home décor, not so much used for scrapbooking and mini albums. I've used my hot glue gun on a lot of crafts with my kids. I don't use it too often when scrapbooking, but it's nice to have to attach special or odd materials together, such as fabric to plastic.

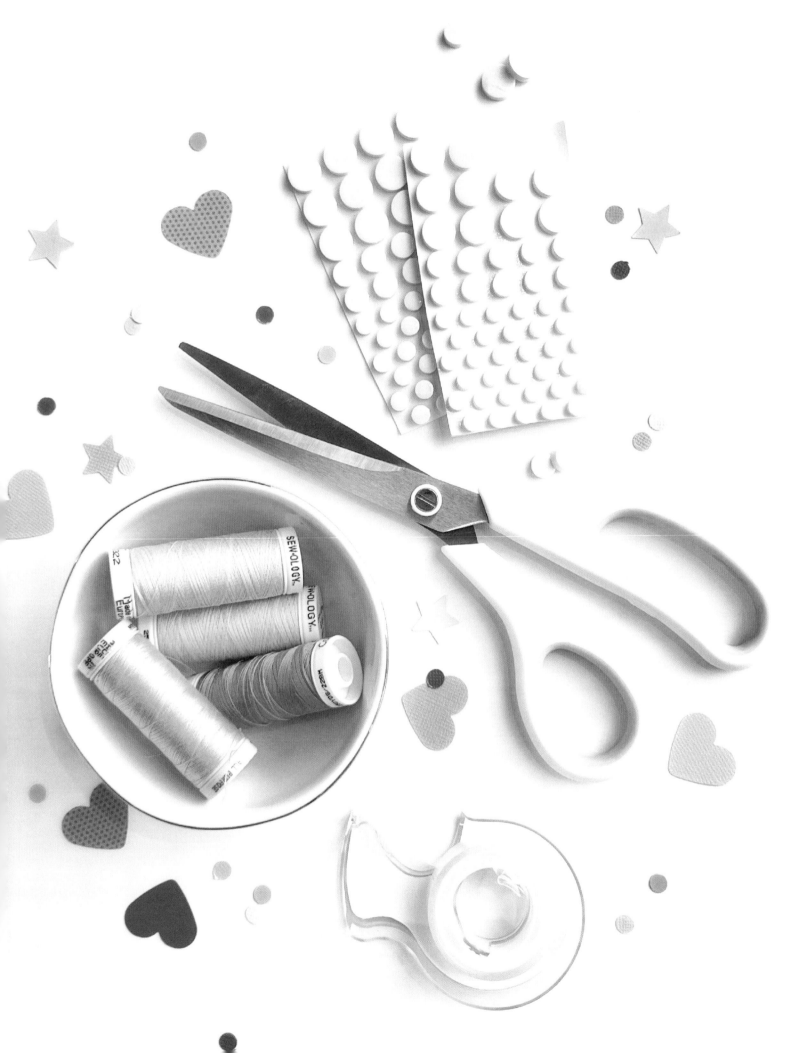

- Similarly, I don't use **superglue** very often, but I have used it to attach magnetic closures for mini albums as well as sticking metal charms back to back. It's not essential to have in your stash, but it can come in useful the times you do need it!

I'm also including staplers under the "adhesives" umbrella because a stapler's main purpose is the same: to attach. A stapler with mini staples is better for crafting—since stickers and embellishments are rather small, a standard stapler is generally too big to really get things stuck in place. You can also get staples in a variety of colors, though I tend to use the standard silver kind.

Electronic Cutting Machine

I purchased a Silhouette Cameo® electronic cutting machine back in 2010, and my scrapbooking hasn't been the same since (in a good way)! The windows and doors that open when you can cut out literally endless amounts of shapes at the touch of a button has elevated my pages like no other tool has. Similar to punches, electronic cutting machines allow you to create a whole bunch of shapes in no time.

The shapes, words, and images that the machine cuts out from your chosen material (such as cardstock, patterned paper, vinyl, vellum, chipboard, etc.) are called cut files (as is the digital file itself, sometimes lengthened to "digital cut file"). I design my own digital cut files and sell them on Etsy, the Silhouette Store, and my own shop. I also have a Cricut® machine, and there are pros and cons to both machines—I don't have a favorite between them. Do your research when shopping for your own cutting machine to figure out which machine might be best for your budget and needs.

Sewing Machine

Another tool that isn't essential but that takes things up a notch is a sewing machine. I purchased the cheapest Brother sewing machine I could find at Wal-Mart back in 2010, and it still works like a charm to this day. I mostly use the running stitches and the zigzag stitches. You can use your sewing machine to attach stickers, papers, and embellishments in place permanently while simultaneously adding texture and a "homespun" look and feel to your pages. I am often inspired by quilts in my scrapbooking (the little fabric pieces translate so perfectly into patterned paper pieces!), so machine stitching only enhances that translation. My tension is set to 2 (I never changed it when I took it out of the box). You can simply use standard thread and needles.

Hand-Stitching Supplies

One technique that I'll never tire of is hand stitching and embroidering on my layouts. It's also the most time consuming of any process—I once spent upward of 48 hours on one layout that included stitching! But the results are so worth it to me.

For hand stitching, you'll need hand-sewing needles, thread and/or embroidery floss, a piercing tool (or a pushpin), and a foam piercing mat. (I bought one of every color of DMC thread, which I store in four compartmentalized plastic storage bins, so that I would always have the perfect color on hand.) You'll often need to pre-pierce holes for stitching, which is where the piercer and mat come in. Place the mat under your paper to both protect your work surface and to give the piercer something to pierce into as you're making the holes.

Endless Extras

Scrapbooking and craft companies are always coming out with the latest and greatest tools to enhance your scrapping. From pink typewriters and sewing machines to button makers and specialty foilers and laminators, there will always be a new tool or toy on the market that you'll want to pick up! Before committing to something, I recommend being sure that you have room to store it and that you'll actually use it. Read reviews and do some homework before jumping on the latest hyped product.

PHOTOGRAPHS

There are many reasons and purposes for scrapbooking. For me, it is a creative outlet, something I enjoy doing, and even a bit of therapy. It helps me stay positive and brings me joy, and I love sharing my results. I love talking about it, teaching about it, and, now, writing about it! At the same time, I am recording our precious memories, documenting our daily lives, and telling our stories. Maybe future generations won't understand it, but in my here and now, it brings light to my life. And it all starts with photos.

You might have an old shoebox of your grandparents' photos that you want to scrapbook to tell their stories. Maybe you have pics of your childhood and good memories that you want to share. Or perhaps you're like me, and your phone is glued to your hip and available at the drop of a hat to snap a photo of something cute your kids or pets or spouse are doing—or even selfies for the win! Whatever the source, photos are the heart of scrapbooking.

Once you have your photos selected, you'll need to print them (if they're not already printed). I recommend printing at home on photo paper (matte or glossy) using a printer that is designed for printing high-quality photos. This way you can control size and cropping easily. Paying for quality products will be reflected in your print quality, so I recommend not scrimping here. If you aren't able to print at home, many scrapbookers use Persnickety Prints to print their photos. Other resources include Wal-Mart, Costco, Amazon, or dozens of other sites. Ask around, find what's in your budget, and get those pics printed!

I tend to use one or two 3" x 4" photos per scrapbook layout and write only a small amount of text.

How Many Photos? How Many Words?

The size and number of photos to use on a single scrapbook page is a hot topic of debate in the scrapbooking world. Some people add lots and lots of photos and lots and lots of journaling, words, and stories. For me, scrapbooking is a form of art and expression. In truth, my photo(s) only get added when the layout is about three-quarters of the way done. I find photos to match my design instead of the other way around. This habit mostly stems from working with companies and needing to feature specific products on my pages—I often create a page focusing on certain colors and elements and then go through my thousands of photos to find the perfect picture to complement the layout. I got so used to scrapbooking this way that I have continued to do it like this, and now, even after 21 years of scrapbooking, I love it more today than I did back then. But your approach to scrapbooking is a completely personal preference—you do you! Do what makes you happy. Just tell your stories and enjoy your process.

I print my photos at about 3" x 4", and I like to add one or two photos per page so that all of the time I spent on my background and details can shine. For mini albums, my photos are usually 2" square. Sometimes I scrap a standard 4" x 6" photo. Sometimes I add more than two photos. I scrap what I want, when I want, with no rules or restrictions, and it's so freeing! Find what works best for you and run with it.

To get different sizes of photos, I use Adobe Photoshop and drag/drop/resize my pictures into a new document to print at home. There are many free photo apps where you can do the same thing and print at home or send to a printer. Some apps even allow you to create collages.

There is also a type of scrapbooking page called a pocket page, which is where you slide photos and journaling cards into page protectors filled with pockets. This method helps tell your stories quickly with not a whole lot of extra embellishing. If you like to finish pages in a relatively short amount of time, this could be a good approach for you.

For mini albums, I use 2" or smaller photos so that there is room for embellishments.

EMBELLISHMENTS

Here comes the really fun part: embellishments! These are the bits and pieces that none of us can get enough of. Stickers. Washi tape. Paper clips. Sequins. Die cuts. Ephemera. All these things make our pages interesting and unique! These can be items that you buy in a collection so they coordinate together perfectly, or they can be items found, saved, and stored that you want to add to help enhance the photo and story you're telling, such as ticket stubs, pamphlets, maps, etc.

I love to use all kinds of embellishments on my pages. The variety of textures, colors, patterns, thicknesses, and materials all combine to create a work of art and love. The pages are tactile, dimensional, colorful, and full of memories.

Mixed media is another aspect of embellishing and includes paints, watercolors, stencils, sprays, texture pastes, gesso, inks, glitter, gelatos, art crayons, stamps, and more! This is a whole other world that I've only recently dipped my toes into, but the results are stunning and always unique. If it's too intimidating for you to try these techniques and media on a full 12" x 12" scrapbook layout, consider beginning on a smaller scale, such as on a gift tag or smaller piece of paper.

STORAGE, ORGANIZATION, AND YOUR SPACE FOR SCRAPPING

In this section we'll go over three important aspects of organization: storing supplies, setting up your workspace, and storing and displaying your finished work. These three areas reflect, in a way, the life cycle of scrapping: from raw materials, to active project, to finished piece. They are all important, and there are things you can do to set yourself up for success no matter the amount of space you have access to.

The space where I scrap truly is my happy scrappy place. Yours should be too!

Storing Crafting Supplies

Storage and organization are almost as important as scrapbooking itself! If it's out of sight, it's usually out of mind, and pretty soon you'll end up with unused supplies galore. Plus, if you spend ten minutes trying to find that certain sticker or that one pretty paper or that super-cute border punch, that's ten minutes you could have spent scrapbooking instead!

First, determine what tools you reach for on a regular basis. For me, that's my paper cutter, scissors, adhesives, and journaling pens and pencils. Keep these in a very accessible place within arm's reach of wherever you're crafting. A rolling cart with shelves and caddies filled with supplies can be handy if you're moving from room to room (for example, bringing your stuff to the dining table to work).

You'll also, of course, need to store tons of paper. Search online and in stores for caddies, organizers, and bins with compartments that can hold 12" x 12" papers. I store cardstock on 12" x 12" wire racks that make it easy to grab the color I want while also acting as a decorative aspect in the room. If you like to work with one collection at a time, try storing the patterned papers alongside their coordinating embellishments in 13" plastic zip-top bags placed vertically in boxes.

Those smaller "eye candy" bits that make the perfect finishing touches on our projects, like brads, buttons, enamel dots, paper clips, and more, are sure to get lost if they're not put away somewhere safe. Find storage with enough compartments to add order to the chaos. But don't feel limited by what you can find at the craft store. Often, makeup or bathroom caddies can be perfect for storing small embellishments—the individual compartments meant for compacts and lipsticks are perfect for die cuts and buttons. Flea markets, antique stores, garage sales, pop-up shops, and craft markets are also great places to keep your eyes peeled for unique and fun storage solutions. I've purchased many jars, plates, cups, and dishes from flea markets to hold charms, buttons, clips, and more.

Sewing-notion boxes are also perfect for keeping teeny tiny scrapbooking embellishments compartmentalized. I have seven of them stacked together in a cubby that are filled with little wood veneer pieces, sequins, paper clips, brads, eyelets, buttons, and so much more. When you need something in one of your boxes, you can simply bring it to your worktable.

One of my biggest storage areas is my 5' x 5' open-backed grid shelving unit. You can find a similar unit in smaller sizes to fit your space too. Fill it up with colorful boxes and baskets full of supplies. I also found a four-tier rotating tray that was silver metal, which I spray-painted gold to match my space better. It holds my sprays, mists, embossing powders, mixed media products, glitter jars, and glazes. Always be on the lookout for items that can be repurposed to your liking.

A Happy Place to Scrap

Whether you have a scrapbook nook, table, niche, corner, room, or an entire wing (hey, one can dream, right?), the place where you scrap and craft should make you happy! For years and years, before I had a dedicated office, I would bring all my craft supplies onto our dining room table and scrap as much as I could before putting it all away again for dinner. In our current home, I took over one room and call it my Happy Scrappy Place, because it is exactly that.

The very first thing I did when we moved into our home was paint my office a pretty shade of robin's-egg blue. It is a great base for my super-colorful room! Consider gray, white, shades of blue, pink, or mint for your space. Wall color makes a big impact on your space and mood. I recommend not going too dark with the color unless you can rely on artificial lighting. Speaking of lighting—make sure you have enough of it, because hours and hours of squinting at little details can take their toll.

I have a few different "stations" in my workplace: the computer desk, the filming table, and the standing desktop. Even if you don't need a filming table, it is great to be able to manipulate and print photos and cut files in the same space as you work, and it's also nice to stand to craft once in a while.

Almost every item in my happy scrappy place has a story behind it. I come from a family of artists. The colorful tassel garlands above my window? My mom made those. The bookcase where I store all my scrapbook magazines and little bits of memorabilia? My dad made it with his own two hands. Almost every inch of wall space in my office is filled with handmade treasures, whether they were made by myself or a friend. Every piece has a story. Every piece is loved and means so much to me. The space where I scrap truly is my happy scrappy place. Yours should be too!

Displaying and Storing Your Projects

Space is not infinite, but after you spend hours working hard on a beautiful memory, the last thing you probably want to do is immediately file it away for it only to be seen on occasion. So try displaying them as I have! I have an ever-changing selection of 35 layouts on one display wall in my scrap room. They're hung on small white nails with clips. As I make new layouts, I switch out older ones; this way, I get to see and enjoy them for much longer than if they all went straight into albums. A few layouts that a lot of love went into have more permanent places on my wall.

Eventually, all my layouts go into 12" x 12" three-ring binder-style scrapbooks. First I slide them in 12" x 12" page protectors and then add them onto the rings. There are different types of albums on the market, ranging in size and material. For example, current albums can come as small as 4" x 4" and go up to 12" x 12", with different sizes in between, with the most popular being 6" x 8", 4" x 8", and 8" x 8". The outer material can be plain fabric, patterned fabric, plastic, or faux leather. I love all the colors and all the patterns, so I don't have any two albums alike!

Once you have full scrapbooks, you can store them on bookshelves in your home alongside books and knickknacks, or in a cabinet dedicated to scrapbooks and photo albums, or anywhere that you like. Try using cabinets with glass doors as I have so that you can see a glimpse of your work and have that pop of color and memory in your space.

In addition to scrapbooking, I also love making mini albums, Coptic books, and home décor pieces. If you're reading this book, I hope to enable you to love making mini albums too! I've found many random furniture pieces throughout the years and upcycled them to store my projects. I spray-painted a three-tiered basket to store all of my beloved mini albums, a child's

box spring to clip on all my handmade cards, and a curio cabinet to hold all my handmade Coptic books. The moral of the story is this: if something is not the right color, you can customize almost anything to a color you love to match your space!

DESIGN

With your photos and supplies in hand, it's time to begin! But how? My key tips are to start with a collection (colors and/or theme), sketch it out, and then seek out inspiration to jump-start your creativity.

Color

When it comes to color and scrapbooking, my best suggestion is to stick with a collection. A collection is a group of supplies designed and released together that all match and carry the same color palette and theme. I release two collections every year; usually, they are "everyday"-themed with bright colors and lots of florals paired with big and bold as well as small and simple designs so things can complement each other.

When faced with a decision of which colors to use in a collection, I usually don't choose—I pick them all! (I often get asked what my favorite color is. The answer is all of them, all the time, always! I suppose if I had to choose a favorite, though, it would be raspberry pink.) Most of my scrapbook layouts are bright, colorful, and have rainbow vibes. That said, it is a fun and creative challenge to narrow your palette to just two or three colors, or even just one color for a monochromatic page.

So, the quick and solid path is to stick to collections where the color work has already been done for you. If you're feeling confident, make your own color collection. Another option is to pick and pull colors from your photos—that way, you have some direction and are sure the photos will gel with the decoration.

Rainbows are my go-to color scheme! Monochromatic looks can be powerful too.

Sketching

Most of the time an idea is just in my head. Sometimes, though, I like to start with a fully drawn-out sketch. You can do this digitally (as I have done) or by hand—it helps to use your ruler so you have an accurate idea of photo sizes. I created a simple document that has twenty $1\,^3/_4$" blank squares that I often print out and use to draw some rudimentary foundation ideas. I can then see the finished page in my mind's eye and go from there. Sometimes a layout will go in a significantly different direction than your original idea, and that's okay—you still have the original idea for a future layout!

There are many online courses based on sketches as well as free sketches that can give you a place to start. I've included a few here for you!

Finding Inspiration

In this day and age, there is inspiration everywhere! Pinterest, Instagram, Facebook, TikTok—you name it, you can garner ideas from it. I get most of my ideas throughout the day as I'm creating. Maya Angelou said, "You can't use up creativity! The more you use, the more you have." I have certainly found that to be true.

However, there are times when I get stuck in a creative rut or get major burnout. If I'm doing too many projects at once, if I'm overwhelmed or stressed, or if I'm anxious or worried or sick, then my creativity goes out the window. But, deep down, I know it's just temporary. The best way I've found to rekindle my creativity is to go outside into nature and take a walk and then just start working immediately afterward. Pull out the papers and supplies, arrange things, start stamping—just getting into the physical act of creating something, even if you don't know what you're doing or have a purpose yet, will usually spark a fire within.

Another potential source of inspiration is to look through past projects and ask yourself, "How can I make this again, but different?" Change the colors. Change the collection. Tweak a little design concept and then re-create the page with those slightly new ideas, and a whole new project is born! We don't always need to reinvent the wheel. Take that pressure off and "scraplift" yourself! Chances are, if you loved the project before, you'll love it again with your new and updated results.

At top is a layout I did when I first started scrapbooking, to remember a trip I took with my husband. Nowadays, I often turn trips into mini albums (middle and bottom), which have more real estate for a variety of photos.

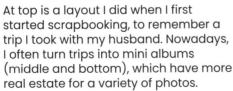

My Favorite Approach: Repetition

My design aesthetic mostly revolves around repetition. I take one idea and repeat it many times to create my page, then add my photo(s) after the background has been created. Here are four example layouts that heavily feature repetition.

Shine Today

For this layout, I took one shape, a triangle, and repeated it several times across the background to create chevrons.

Last Day of School

The repeated element on this page is stars. I took one star shape and repeated it in increasing sizes to create a focal design element on the background.

I Love to Create

Fringed paper strips are the element that I repeated to create this super-textured and colorful background.

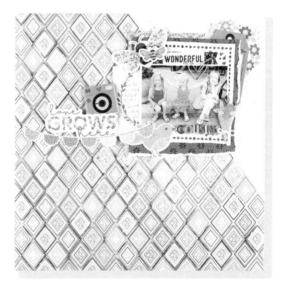

Cousins

Diamonds are the repeating shape on this layout. I cut a bunch of them out, distressed the edges, and then adhered them back on top of a second piece of the same diamond paper for a dimensional and interesting background.

SCRAPBOOK LAYOUTS

This is what you're here for—so many scrapbook layout ideas that you're sure to be busy for weeks! Each of the nine layouts includes different techniques, fun details, and bonus examples to serve as endless inspiration.
I can't wait to see what you make!

BORDER PUNCHES

Border punches are a tool that I always keep an eye out for any time I go to the craft store. There are many beautiful and varied designs and so many unique ways to use them! Layering punched paper strips down and across or all over a page is one of my favorite techniques and looks beautiful no matter what. Metal dies, cut files, and deco scissors can also be used to achieve similar results—there's no right or wrong way to create these paper strips! So grab those border punches and let's make a layout.

SUPPLIES

- Photo: (1) 3" x 4"
- Neutral cardstock (for page base)
- Cardstock
- Patterned papers
- Assortment of border punches
- Liquid adhesive
- Sewing machine (optional)
- Rainbow of threads (optional)
- Stickers
- Embellishments
- White acrylic paint
- Paintbrush
- Journaling die cut
- Journaling pen

FINISHED SIZE: 12" SQUARE

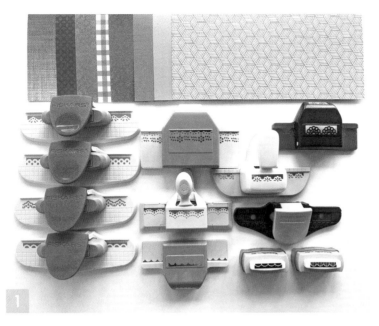

STEP 1: **Choose papers and punches.**
Begin with an assortment of border punches and patterned papers or cardstock sheets. Alternatively, you can use just one or two for a unified look. I chose a collection of warm-toned, mostly solid-toned patterned papers. Change up the colors and patterns for a whole new look!

STEP 2: **Punch one strip.** Align your paper or cardstock at the top of the punch and press the punch. Move the paper over so it aligns with the pattern printed on the punch and press the punch again. Continue moving, aligning, and punching until you have about 12" of paper (typically, the whole width of the paper) punched.

STEP 3: **Cut the strip.** Trim off the punched edge using a paper trimmer.

STEP 4: **Punch the rest of the strips.** Repeat making these punched paper strips using various punch designs from various patterned papers until you have about 25–30 strips. Align the strips in the order you want them to appear on your layout.

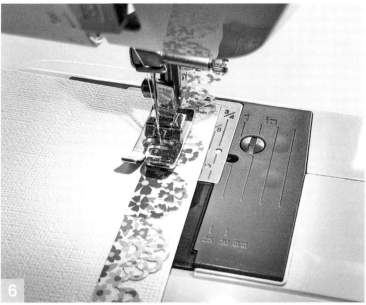

STEP 5: Glue the first strip. Grab a neutral cardstock for the page base. Starting at the bottom, grab the bottom paper strip, flip it over, add a line of liquid adhesive across the top of the strip, and then glue it down at the bottom of the cardstock, leaving some free space to its left side.

STEP 6: Stitch the strip. If desired, use a coordinating color of thread to machine-stitch across the top of the paper strip to attach it in place permanently and create even more texture.

STEP 7: Glue the remaining strips. Continue gluing and stitching paper strips from the bottom all the way up to the top of the page. Overlap some of the strips a little bit as shown, and always glue each strip with some free space to the left side of the layout. Change thread colors with the changing colors of paper.

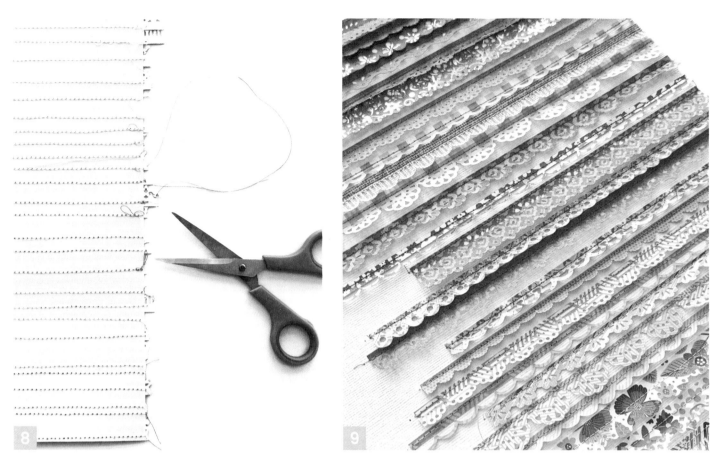

STEP 8: Trim the strips and threads. Trim off the excess paper ends hanging off the right edge of the layout as well as the excess thread ends. Don't forget to trim the threads on the back side.

STEP 9: Bend the strips. Bend up the long edges of the paper strips to add dimension and shadows.

STEP 10: Add embellishments. Start adding embellishments tone on tone on top of the paper strips. Once you like the placement of them, secure them in place permanently with liquid adhesive.

STEP 11: Add paint splatters. For another layer of interest, splash watered-down white acrylic paint across the entire page. This step creates cohesiveness and an interesting effect.

STEP 12: Add the photo and title. Place a 3" x 4" photo on the left side, overlapping the edges of that section of paper strips, then add a title sticker over a less important part of the photo.

STEP 13: Add journaling. Tuck a journaling die cut under the left side of the photo, then write the story with a coordinating pen color to finish.

Cozy

Central Focus

This layout is very similar to the featured layout, except the border-punched paper strips are shorter and staggered down the center of the page.

I Think You Are Pretty Amazing

Aligned Left

This is also quite similar to the featured layout, but with a lighter color palette and with the strips placed down the left side instead of the right side. You don't always need to reinvent the wheel. If there is a technique you love, use it often! By simply changing one or two things, you can get a completely new page with stunning results.

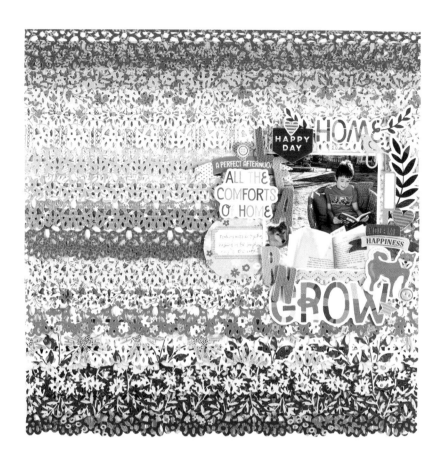

Grow

Full, Consistent Coverage

For this page, I used the same border punch to make all the paper strips and layered them down the entire background with no white space showing. A cluster of embellishments, including the title and journaling centered around the photo, helps draw your eye to the picture despite the busier background.

Party Store Adventures

Punched Strips Shape

Instead of covering part of the background directly, I cut a large heart from cardstock, covered it with border-punched paper strips, then trimmed the excess around the entire heart to make it into a large focal shape on my page. A smattering of paints on the darker background helps tie all the colors together, and I journaled right onto the background.

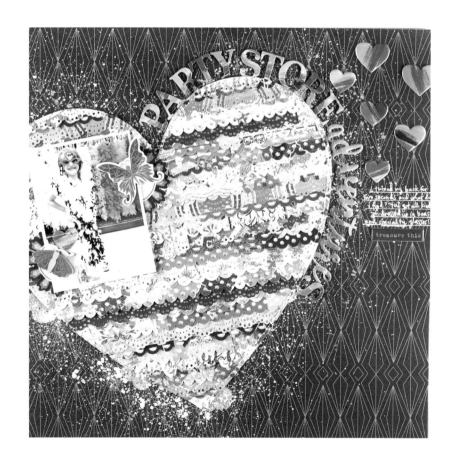

MIXED MEDIA

Paints, sprays, inks, glitter, gesso, stencils, acrylics, watercolors—all these media and more can be combined to create a mixed media layout. The variety can be messy, so always have scrap paper, wipes, and water nearby to clean up. If you're feeling intimidated by the thought of trying mixed media on a full 12" x 12" layout, start small and experiment on tags or mini pages. Then you can even incorporate those finished tags onto a full-page layout!

SUPPLIES

- Photos: (4) 3" square
- White cardstock (*for page base*)
- Stencil
- Modeling paste
- Spatula
- Watercolors
- Paintbrush
- White acrylic paint
- Sewing machine

- White thread
- Cardstock
- Patterned papers
- Foam squares
- Adhesives
- Stickers (*including alphabet stickers*)
- Journaling die cut
- Journaling pen
- Tab sticker

FINISHED SIZE: 12" SQUARE

STEP 1: **Prepare to stencil.** Place scrap paper on your work surface to keep it clean, since mixed media can be messy business. Grab a piece of smooth white cardstock, a stencil, modeling paste, and a spatula.

STEP 2: **Stencil one quadrant.** Set the stencil on the top left quadrant of the cardstock and gently scrape modeling paste through it, using the spatula, until as much or as little of the stencil is covered as you desire.

STEP 3: **Stencil a second quadrant.** Carefully lift up the stencil. Place it on the bottom left section of the cardstock and repeat scraping modeling paste through it.

STEP 4: **Finish stenciling.** Repeat for the last two quadrants of the background until all four sections have been stenciled. Let the paste dry completely—you can speed up the drying process with a hair dryer.

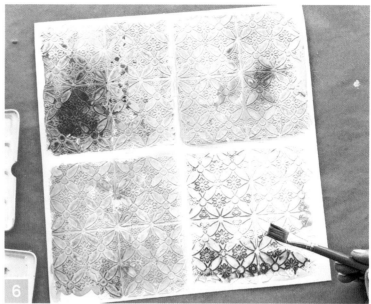

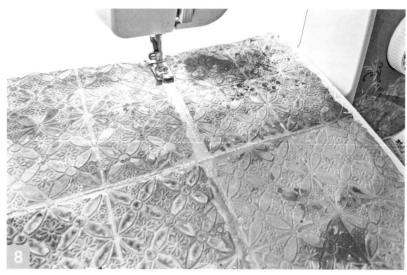

STEP 5: Paint the stenciled areas. Grab watercolors, a cup of water, and a paintbrush. Paint each of the four sections a different color using one or two shades of the same color of watercolor for each section (such as a dark and light pink). Let the colors bleed and blend into each other to create a beautiful background.

STEP 6: Add watercolor splatters. Splash a shade of the same color on top of its corresponding section to create another layer of paint shapes and interest. Repeat the process for each of the four quadrants.

STEP 7: Add acrylic splatters. Once the background has dried, splash a final layer of watered-down white acrylic paint over the whole thing. Let it dry.

STEP 8: Stitch between the quadrants. Machine-stitch with white thread and a basic running stitch between the quadrants of stenciling both vertically and horizontally.

STEP 9: Cut photo backgrounds. At first, I was only planning to use two photos, but eventually I ended up using four. Trim four patterned papers in four coordinating colors to 3 ½" square—slightly larger all around than the photos.

STEP 10: Distress additional photo backgrounds. Grab some additional patterned papers and rip or heavily distress the edges with scissors or your fingernail to reveal the white core. Attach the paper squares and distressed pieces in place with foam squares. (I've found foam squares are one of the only types of adhesive that will stick to mixed media.)

STEP 11: Add fussy-cut flowers. Add additional layers of torn and distressed papers to some of the quadrants. Fussy-cut flowers from patterned papers to tuck into the paper layers.

STEP 12: Embellish. Start embellishing! Grab stickers, sentiments, die cuts, and more that go along with your theme and story and layer them on, under, and around the photos. Choose some pieces that are tone on tone and others that are contrasting for a fun, varied, and very colorful page.

STEP 13: Finish the title. Complete the title with the addition of mini alphabet stickers.

STEP 14: Finish embellishing. Sprinkle in some of your tiniest embellishments last to fill in any gaps and create final bits of interest and eye candy.

STEP 15: Add journaling. Journal the story with a pen on a journaling die cut tucked into the mix. Write the date on a tab sticker and insert it near the top.

Love You

Layers upon Layers

I had so much fun adding layers, layers, and more layers to this layout! First gesso, then modeling paste scraped through a heart stencil, topped with watercolors, then hearts punched from patterned papers, layered, and machine-stitched in place, with a final layer of die-cut letters that I hand-stitched through. All the layers and textures and colors combine to create a beautiful page documenting my darling daughter.

XOXO

Busy Painted and Stenciled Background

Sometimes a background can look like a hot mess, but the more you add, the more it starts to come together. Just go with it! Cluster your photo, title, journaling, date, and embellishments together so your eye has somewhere to focus instead of the busy background.

Always Love You

Spray-Colored Hearts and Glitter

This is another layout with a whole bunch of layers. The first step was painting variegated black stripes down the middle. Can you spot some glitter in the mix? I don't always add glitter, but when I do, it sure makes for some sparkle and shine! To make the hearts on top, I spritzed a piece of white cardstock with all kinds of colored sprays, then punched three sizes of hearts from the entire background. I layered three concentric hearts together, machine-stitched through them, and added them with foam squares atop the mixed media background.

Relax

Rips and Strips Galore

Mixed media is about trying new things, experimenting, and using different media and techniques on a single page. This page includes many of the previously mentioned techniques, plus border-punched paper strips and fussy-cut butterflies. It looked a little scary at first, but I just kept going, adding more layers, and the photos helped ground it. The moral of the story is, don't be afraid of all that's going on—just keep at it, and then eventually make a focal point with photos.

It was so special to have my mom here on Mother's Day 2022!

SUCH A GOOD DAY

STAMPING

Stamps come in many forms; the most popular are wood-mounted rubber stamps, acrylic stamps, and roller stamps. They're fun to collect, organize, and—of course—use to make pretty things! One awesome aspect of stamps is you can never run out of them—you can literally use the same stamp forever, and you'll still have it. That makes stamps great for creating multiples, which is ideal for making cards in bulk. For scrapbooking, it's a perfect technique for creating repetition.

SUPPLIES

- Photos: (1) 3" x 4", (1) 4" x 3"
- Colored cardstock (for page base)
- Acrylic stamps
- Acrylic block
- Eraser
- Rainbow of stamping inks

- White cardstock
- Liquid adhesive
- Patterned papers
- White acrylic paint
- Paintbrush
- Sequins
- Stickers
- White journaling pen

FINISHED SIZE: 12" SQUARE

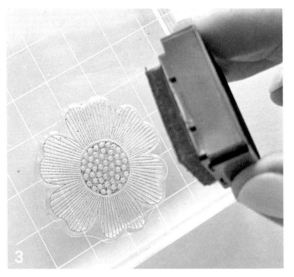

STEP 1: Collect your stamping supplies. To begin, grab a set of acrylic stamps, a rainbow of inks, an acrylic block, an eraser, and a piece of smooth white cardstock.

STEP 2: Prep the stamp. The first time you use an acrylic stamp, you need to prep the stamp for ink by rubbing an eraser over it. Dust off any eraser remnants, then it's ready to go!

STEP 3: Add ink. Place the stamp on the acrylic block and choose your ink color. Dab the ink onto the stamp until it's completely and evenly covered.

STEP 4: Stamp once. It's important to place something squishy, like a magazine or foam board, under the smooth white cardstock before stamping. Then turn the acrylic block over and press the stamp, with even distribution of force, down onto the cardstock.

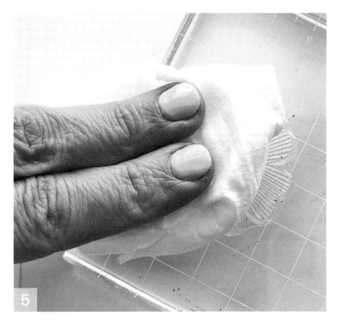

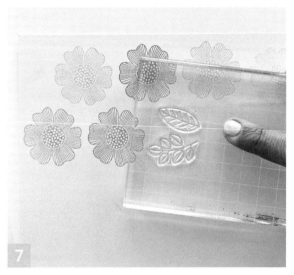

STEP 5: Stamp more times with different colors. If you are changing colors of ink, wipe off the stamp to make it clean. Repeat inking, stamping, and cleaning for as many motifs as you'd like to make.

STEP 6: Finish stamping one motif. I created about 31 flowers for my page. It's always a good idea to make more than you think you'll need—if you don't use them all, you can just add the extras to your collection of miscellaneous leftovers for future projects.

STEP 7: Change motifs. Once you're finished with one image (in this case, a flower), remove the stamp from the acrylic block, put it back with its stamp set, and grab the next image (in this case, two leaves). Prep the leaves with an eraser, then ink, stamp, clean, and repeat until you have as many motifs as you'd like.

STEP 8: Fussy-cut the motifs. Fussy-cut all the stamped flowers and leaves from the cardstock with a fine-tipped pair of scissors. Give life and dimension to the flowers and leaves by gently pinching and creasing the petals and edges.

STEP 9: **Arrange and glue the flowers.** Choose a patterned paper or cardstock background and place the stamped flowers across the middle without adhering them in place yet. Once you like your arrangement, take a quick photo to refer back to. Then add just a dab of liquid adhesive to the back of each flower to attach each one in place—this lets the petals lift off the page and keep their intended dimension.

STEP 10: **Cut the stem strips.** Trim ⅛" strips of green patterned papers for stems. Decide on an order you like. I alternated light and dark green.

STEP 11: **Glue the stem strips.** Glue and tuck the stems in place up underneath the flowers. Trim the excess that extends beyond the bottom of the page.

STEP 12: **Glue the leaves.** Glue the leaves beside the stems to complete the flower garden look.

STEP 13: **Splatter on some paint.** Create a cohesive layer by splashing watered-down white acrylic paint all over the page. Let it dry.

STEP 14: **Add the photos.** Tuck two photos under the flowers on the top left side of the page. Glue them down.

STEP 15: **Add embellishments.** Embellish most of the flower centers with a sequin or flower sticker. Leave some flower centers empty for balance.

STEP 16: **Add a title and journaling.** Add a sentiment sticker for the title on the right edge of the right photo, tuck a floral border sticker underneath it, and then add journaling with a white pen above the title to finish the layout.

Happiness

Layered-Color Stamps

There are so very many absolutely beautiful stamps on the market! This floral heart, which was designed by my good friend and owner of A Pocket Full of Happiness (a scrapbooking store), spoke to me, and I had to use it right away! Each flower heart is made up of four different color layers, so it was fun to put together an array of color palettes. I couldn't possibly pick a favorite color combination—they're all my favorite, and they look beautiful all together!

You Make My Heart Flutter

Single-Stamp Custom Background

I grabbed a single butterfly stamp and a rainbow of ink colors, then, starting at the bottom left and working my way up to the top right, I stamped the butterflies in all the colors of ink to create my own custom patterned background. To go along with the theme of butterflies, I topped the page with butterfly stickers and butterfly die cuts.

You Make My Heart Happy

Realistic Layered-Color Stamps

Here is another example of a layout made with layered stamps, this time with coordinating metal dies. That is, I used a manual die cut machine to cut out the flower bases from smooth white cardstock, and then I used the coordinating pieces of the stamp to layer the realistic-looking design on top. It is a lengthy process to make this many flowers and leaves, but the results are always stunning!

So Totes Adorbs

Inked and Watercolored Stamps

Stamping ink isn't the only option available for stamping! For this layout, I used butterfly stamps and watercolors. I love the varied and transparent layers this technique creates. It took some time to cut out every butterfly and then stitch through it with a matching color of thread, but I love how it turned out.

LARGE TITLE

At a loss for where to begin? How about with a large title? A large title as an anchor and focal point makes it easy to simply add photos and embellishments around it. Large titles take up most of the space of a layout, and you'll always end up with oh-so-stunning results! There are many ways to create large titles, from using cut files or individual large letters to using ransom-style hand-cut letters or many other techniques. A large title is a great way to express a statement and make a big impact.

SUPPLIES

- Photos: (3) 3" x 4"
- Colored cardstock *(for page base)*
- "LOVE GROWS HERE" digital cut file
- Electronic cutting machine
- Textured white cardstock
- Additional cardstock
- Patterned papers
- Pencil
- Liquid adhesive
- Foam squares
- Stickers *(including a banner label)*
- Roller date stamp
- Stamping ink
- White journaling pen

FINISHED SIZE: 12" SQUARE

STEP 1: Prep the cut file. Use an electronic cutting machine to cut out a large "LOVE GROWS HERE" title from textured white cardstock at about 11" x 7". Save all the inner letter pieces.

STEP 2: Choose backings. Choose 12 mostly solid-patterned papers or colorful cardstock sheets to back the cut file. This is a great project for utilizing scraps! Place the inner letter pieces on top of the patterned papers to figure out the order in which you want the backings to appear.

STEP 3: Trace the first letter or motif. Flip both the inner piece of the cut file and the chosen patterned paper over, then trace the shape with a pencil onto the patterned paper.

STEP 4: Cut out the letter or motif. Cut out the traced shape about $1/8$" larger than the pencil lines so you can add adhesive onto it to attach it to the back of the cut file. If you cut it out to the exact same size, along your tracing lines, the patterned paper piece will fall right through the cut file and won't have anything to grab on to.

STEP 5: Cut out the remaining letters. Repeat the tracing/cutting process for all 12 letters and motifs.

STEP 6: Glue the inner letter hole pieces. Use liquid adhesive to glue the inner letter hole pieces to the fronts of their corresponding cut-out letters. In this case, there are just two: the holes in each of the "R" letters.

STEP 7: Glue a few letters at a time. Add liquid adhesive onto the back of two or three letters of the white sentiment cut file at a time, then place the cut-out patterned paper letters in their coordinating spots.

STEP 8: Flip it over to reveal the result. Once all the letters are in place, flip the sentiment over and admire your work! The big reveal is the best part of backing a cut file.

STEP 9: **Attach the sentiment.** Choose a solid-patterned paper or cardstock for the background and attach the cut file at the top using foam squares for dimension and to create shadows. Since scrapbooking with flat papers is by nature two-dimensional, adding foam squares helps create depth and interest.

STEP 10: **Add photos.** Tuck three photos underneath the large title. Glue them down.

STEP 11: **Start embellishing.** Begin embellishing with chipboard flower stickers under and on top of the title. Consider trimming larger floral stickers and wreaths in half and tucking them on opposite sides of the title to create symmetry.

STEP 12: **Add more stickers.** Next, bring in cardstock stickers and continue adding other embellishments to give life to your page.

STEP 13: **Add the date.** Stamp the date on a banner label sticker and tuck it under the title.

STEP 14: **Add journaling.** Add journaling with a white pen under the right photo.

STEP 15: **Add final details.** I felt the page needed just one last touch—so I placed two gold heart stickers near opposite edges of the page to finish it.

Love This Girl
Hand-Cut Letters

This layout has a similar vibe to the featured layout with its large title and flowers galore, but this time I didn't back a cut file—instead, I simply used larger letters and popped them off the pink background with foam squares. I almost always add interest to my flower die cuts by pinching the petals to give them a lifelike look.

Best Day Ever
Stitched Sequin Title

This layout was a labor of love! I glued sequins into a large title shape and then hand-stitched them all in place. This layout, unlike many of my layouts, is monochromatic: almost every element is a tint, tone, or shade of blue! That makes the layout all about texture and the different materials, including paper, plastic, cardstock, and chipboard.

Love Love Love

Peekaboo Photos and Journaling

This is one of those layout designs that I repeat with almost every scrapbook collection. Just by changing the papers, it's a whole new look! I die-cut "LOVE" three times (each letter from a different patterned paper), distressed the edges for texture, and then adhered them with foam squares onto a mixed media background. Letter "O"s make great frames for photos as well as spots for journaling.

I Must Have Flowers Always and Always

Ransom Note Title

Have you ever tried hand-cutting letters from magazines or patterned papers for a ransom note look? That's exactly what I did here! Large titles can also be long titles made with smaller letters that still fill up almost an entire background. Then you just tuck your photos into the design. Distressing the edges of every letter, while a bit time consuming, helps create a defining edge and makes them pop from the light-colored background. I topped this design off with machine stitching to double as another texture and to keep the letters in place.

GRID

A grid design helps break down a full page into smaller, more manageable sections. There are many techniques for creating the initial grid, such as using paper strips, machine-stitched lines, washi tape, hand-stitched dividers, paper weaving, or cut files. Once the grid is in place, it's a bit like a puzzle to fill in and connect all the pieces! You can also vary the size and number of sections, from large ones like 2" x 2" all the way up to 8" x 8" and beyond. The possibilities with grids are virtually limitless, and even a simple grid concept can be reworked into new and brilliant results with minor changes.

SUPPLIES

- Photos: (5) 2" square
- Purple cardstock *(for page base)*
- Patterned papers
- Pencil
- Ruler
- Liquid adhesive
- Sewing machine *(optional)*

- White thread *(optional)*
- Stickers
- Die cuts
- Lined die cut
- Journaling pen
- Enamel dots

FINISHED SIZE: 12" SQUARE

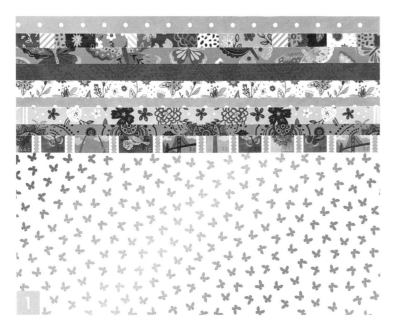

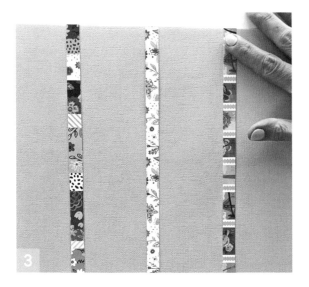

STEP 1: Cut six strips. Many patterned papers come with a ½" barcode strip across the top or bottom of the full 12" x 12" sheet and feature information on one side and a pattern on the opposite side. These make for fun and creative uses! Cut six barcode strips (or simply six ½" x 12" strips of patterned paper).

STEP 2: Mark the page base. On a sheet of purple cardstock, use a ruler and pencil to measure and mark at 3", 6", and 9" on all four edges.

STEP 3: Glue the first three strips. Figure out the desired placement of your paper strips (three vertical and three horizontal). Flip over the three vertical strips, add a dab of liquid adhesive at the top, and press them at the top edge of the cardstock, centered on the pencil marks.

STEP 4: Insert the fourth strip. Grab the first horizontal strip and weave it over, under, and over the three vertical strips. Add a dab of glue on the top pencil mark on the left edge and press the end of the horizontal strip in place.

STEP 5: Insert the remaining strips. Weave the middle horizontal paper strip under, over, and under, then glue it in place at the middle left pencil mark. Repeat for the bottom paper strip but weave it over, under, and over. Glue down all the loose strip ends (for vertical and horizontal strips).

STEP 6: Stitch the strips. For another layer of texture, use a sewing machine with white thread and a basic running stitch to stitch down the center of every paper strip.

STEP 7: Trim the threads. Trim excess thread ends. Don't worry about your gluing or stitching being perfect—embrace the imperfections in scrapbooking. We're only human, after all, and we're creating with our own two hands!

STEP 8: Finish the grid. Pinch and bend up the edges of the paper strips to turn the flat and two-dimensional background grid into an interesting three-dimensional one.

STEP 9: Add the photos. Place and glue five photos into the empty sections.

STEP 10: Add halved flowers. Trim flower die cuts or stickers in half and tuck them under the edges of the paper strips to create an effect of them growing out of the strips.

STEP 11: Add more flowers. For individual flowers, give them lifelike dimension by pinching the petals before tucking them into place. You can see on the back side of this flower how I creased each petal.

STEP 12: Embellish. Continue adding additional flower stickers, sentiment stickers, and other small embellishments to decorate all but one of the sections of the grid.

STEP 13: Add journaling. Journal on a lined die cut and add it to the empty section.

STEP 14: Add final touches. Save tiny stickers, small sentiments, and enamel dots for the final embellishments to fill in any empty spaces and finish off little clusters of decoration.

Born to Create

Tiny Grid

This page technique is identical to the featured layout in design but uses 16 thinner paper strips instead of six. This creates many tinier spaces in the grid, so I filled in almost every little space with a small embellishment and only used two large photos on top instead of five in individual spaces. This is one of the layouts I taught in one of my very first virtual layout classes!

Sunshine

Heart Grid with Peekaboo Photos

Shapes make for great grid designs too! This hearts background is one of my cut files. I added mixed media and hand stitching, backed most sections with patterned papers, and then machine-stitched the whole thing onto a white cardstock background. The empty hearts are perfect spots for photos.

Feels Like Home

Stitched Grid

Instead of woven paper strips as in the featured layout, here I've machine-stitched the initial 5 x 5 grid with white thread and a basic running stitch. Every space is filled with either a photo or a 2" x 2" piece of paper. Many of my designer scrapbook collections come with 2" x 2" paper pads, and this grid technique is an excellent option for using them! Take things to the next level by adding hand-stitched details to shapes and phrases on the papers.

Cool

Circle Grid with Standout Words

This layout is another example of a nonlinear grid design made of circles instead of squares; it also features one of my cut files. The technique is like the Sunshine heart grid example at left, but slight tweaks make for completely different results! I embellished this layout tone on tone for fun texture and with a different scrapbook collection with a drastically different color scheme.

QUILT INSPIRED

One of my favorite starting points for scrapbook layouts is browsing through quilts on Pinterest. The little fabric shapes translate so easily into patterned paper pieces and can often be created with the help of a punch. I can't tell you how many layouts I've made by first punching squares and then cutting them in half diagonally to create triangles. The number of quilts that are made up of different arrangements of triangles is endless, and they all work perfectly for piecing pages together! Size your square punch up or down for more fabulous results. It's one of my goals to see how many pages I can create with a simple square punch. In addition to punches, hand stitching and machine stitching also evoke quilt-like vibes, so I often use those techniques when working on quilt-inspired pages.

SUPPLIES

- Photos: (5) 2" square
- Blue cardstock (*for page base*)
- Patterned papers
- 1" square punch
- Ruler
- Adhesive of choice
- Sewing machine (*optional*)
- White thread (*optional*)
- Die cuts
- Alphabet stickers
- Additional stickers
- Chipboard button stickers
- Enamel dots
- Journaling pen
- Roller date stamp
- Stamping ink

FINISHED SIZE: 12" SQUARE

STEP 1: Choose your quilt papers. Collect a whole bunch of patterned papers. This is a great layout for using up paper scraps. You can also choose a limited color palette—I used papers from my Splendid collection, which has many more colors in the palette, but I opted for only orange, yellow, green, and blue papers.

STEP 2: Punch the squares. Use a 1" square to punch fifty 1" squares.

STEP 3: Cut the triangles. Cut each paper square in half diagonally to make triangles. Save time by stacking three or four squares together and cutting the stack with regular scissors.

STEP 4: Glue the first triangle. Choose a piece of cardstock or solid-patterned paper for the layout background. Beginning on the bottom left corner, attach a paper triangle with a little dab of lightweight or temporary adhesive if you're planning to add machine stitching, or permanent adhesive if you're not going to add machine stitching.

STEP 5: **Finish the first pinwheel.** Place three more paper triangles around the first one in a pinwheel pattern.

STEP 6: **Complete the bottom row.** Continue adding four paper triangles at a time in pinwheel fashion in a row across the entire bottom of the page.

STEP 7: **Complete the left column.** Move up to above your first pinwheel and create pinwheels of triangles all the way up the left side of the page.

STEP 8: **Finish adding pinwheels.** Continue adding paper triangles as shown, adding more or fewer as desired until you are happy with your design.

STEP 9: Machine-stitch the triangles. Once the background looks the way you want it to, if desired, use a sewing machine with white thread and a zigzag stitch to stitch horizontally, vertically, and in both directions diagonally across the triangles to really drive home the quilt inspiration.

STEP 10: Trim threads. Trim excess thread ends. Don't worry about threads potentially unraveling a bit after they are cut—it's all part of the handmade nature, and attempting to glue them securely would just turn into a sticky mess!

STEP 11: Add the photos. Place two photos overlapping and at slight angles for whimsy and interest over the top right section of the paper pinwheels. Don't glue them yet.

STEP 12: Add die cuts. Layer and tuck various die cuts under and over the photos to create a cluster, a single large, grounding element for your eyes. Adhere everything in place.

STEP 13: Create a title. Make a title with an assortment of sentiment stickers and colorful alphabet stickers next to the right photo.

STEP 14: Add stickers. Add chipboard button stickers and enamel dots tone on tone to some of the paper triangles for more texture and interest.

STEP 15: Add journaling and the date. Add journaling on a lined die cut that is tucked under the left photo. Stamp the date on a label sticker to finish.

So Much Love for You

Quilted Cut File

For this layout, I featured a quilt cut file and backed all the triangular sections with patterned papers and the squares/diamonds with photos or filled them with handwritten journaling. I placed the papers in a random rainbow order, but an alternative idea is to place them in a more stylized order, such as ombre, warm to cool, light to dark, etc. This layout is very balanced—it's almost completely symmetrical in multiple directions.

You Rock

Border Journaling

This layout also features a cut file, but this one is made up completely of triangles. I used the same 1" square punch as in the featured layout to punch dozens of squares, cut them into triangles, and used those to back the cut file. It was time consuming, but, as I've said and I'm sure I'll say again, I love projects where I can use my two hands to turn papers into works of art! A photo smack dab in the center with layers of die cuts and sentiments draws the eye right in, and journaling around the border is a fun placement.

A Little Us Time at Home

Hand-Stitched Color Transitions

There are many quilt-inspired patterned papers in my collections that are made up of triangles or little sections of patterns. For this page, I hand-stitched with a matching color of embroidery thread around each and every triangle to really enhance the quilt theme. I didn't want to cover up too much of the stitching, so I centered my photo and embellishments in the middle with a little caption written below to tell the story of snuggles at home with the kids and kitties.

Virtual Playdate

Layered Oval Pattern

I love using two of the same paper to create supremely textured pages. I left the first patterned paper background as is. For the second, I used a circle punch to punch out all the inner white spaces between the patterns, then stitched them in place in the same spot on the first paper layer. Once I finished the machine stitching, I bent up all the edges of the petals to create oh so much texture and interest! As with most of the other example layouts, the photo is in the very center to ground the page and create a visual resting place.

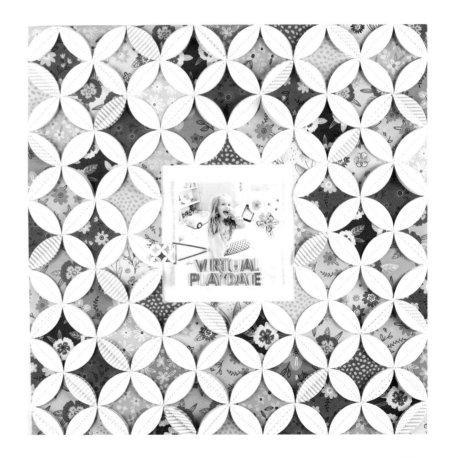

FLOWER WREATH

Oh my goodness: flowers. My favorite shape/icon ever to work with in scrapbooking. You won't find many of my layouts lacking flowers, and they are always a prominent feature in my signature scrapbooking collections! Now, don't ask me if I can keep actual flowers alive . . . I do not have a green thumb. But paper flowers? I am so there, and I love making them! Anytime I can create a flower or use a flower, I almost certainly will. I hope to inspire you with these floral pages.

SUPPLIES

- Photo: (1) 3" x 4"
- White cardstock *(for page base)*
- Pencil
- Paper plate, compass, or 8" circle template
- Paintbrush
- Watercolors
- Flower die cuts
- Liquid adhesive
- Letter stickers
- Additional stickers *(hearts or desired elements)*
- Tab sticker
- Journaling pen
- Roller date stamp
- Stamping ink
- Flower charms
- Glue dots

FINISHED SIZE: 12" SQUARE

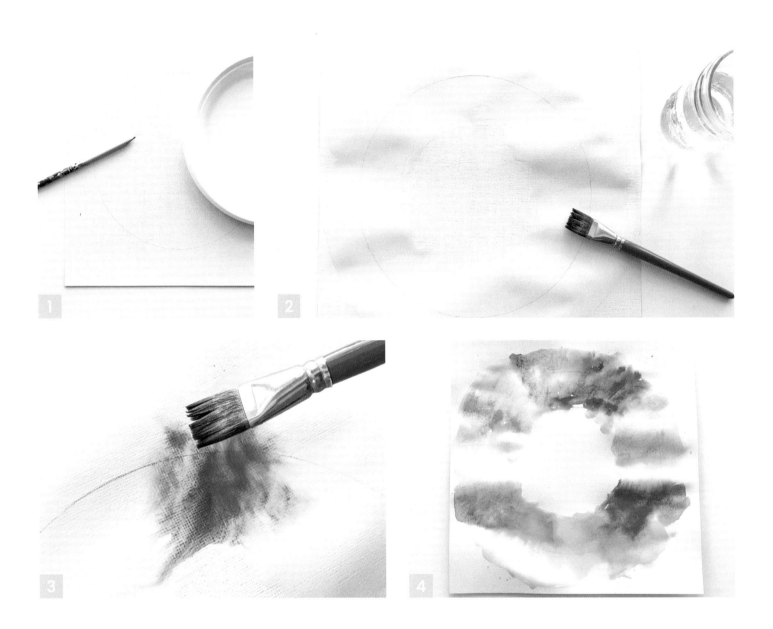

STEP 1: Trace a circle. Use a pencil and a paper plate (or other circle template) to trace a circle onto the center of a white cardstock background.

STEP 2: Wet the circle. With a paintbrush, drop generous amounts of water all over the drawn circle.

STEP 3: Add watercolors. Immediately, while the water is still wet, drop different watercolor shades into the wet circle one color at a time, letting the colors bleed and blend together.

STEP 4: Finish watercoloring. I dropped my paints in rainbow order, but you could also choose a different colorway for a completely new look!

STEP 5: Crease the flowers. Gather a bunch of flower and leaf die cuts, then start pinching and creasing the petals and center veins to add dimension. This will give them a realistic vibe.

STEP 6: Finish prepping. While the background dries, finish creasing all the die cuts. Once it's dry, the background will probably be very wrinkly. If you want it to be flatter (totally optional), leave it under something heavy overnight or run it through a laminating machine in a protective sleeve a few times.

STEP 7: Place the flowers. Begin placing the flowers and leaves, matching up the die cuts' colors with the colors of the background so that pink flowers are on a pink section, green leaves are on a green section, etc. Don't glue anything down yet.

STEP 8: Take a reference photo. Once you are happy with the placement of all the elements, take a picture to refer to as you continue working.

STEP 9: Glue down the flowers. Add a dab of liquid adhesive to the center back of every die cut so the petals can still lift off the page. You can glue one at a time, a section at a time, or however you like.

STEP 10: Add the photo. Tuck a photo into the center of the wreath so that some petals or leaves overlap it and help incorporate it into the overall design. Glue it down.

STEP 11: Add a title. Spell out a title by adding letter stickers overlapping one side of the photo and in the empty space remaining in the center. Put some heart stickers in any gaps.

STEP 12: Add journaling. Journal below the title with a color of pen that matches the nearby section of flowers.

STEP 13: Stamp the date. Stamp the date on a tab sticker and place it above the title.

STEP 14: Add charms. Use glue dots to attach flower charms into the wreath, again placing them tone on tone.

14

She Makes

Tiny Cut Flower Wreath

This layout uses a flower punch set and a single piece of patterned paper. I punched out nearly the entire piece of patterned paper to get the various flowers, layered them together, then placed them in a round wreath arrangement framing a central photo. I love the simpler color palette of this layout. And—if it wasn't clear—I love flowers. In all varieties— paper, sequin, sticker—all the flowers, always!

Family

Big Blossom Floral Frame

For this layout, I used metal dies and a manual die cut machine along with red, pink, yellow, green, blue, and purple monochromatic cardstocks. I also die-cut teeny tiny flowers and the title from white cardstock to create more of a textured element on the white cardstock background. Since the floral frame took many hours to complete, I didn't want to add too much else—a photo and a caption in the center wrapped it up. I can feel my love for my family through the love that went into making this layout!

Me and My Girl
Rainbow Button Wreath

To make these flowers, I used a heart punch and a rainbow array of patterned papers. Each flower requires eight larger hearts and eight smaller hearts, each folded in half and then adhered onto a round scrap of paper. (Check out the process video on my YouTube channel—they're fun and addicting to make!) After making the nine flowers, I adhered them in my go-to rainbow wreath design. Hopefully you can see how the same idea with just a simple tweak here and there can look completely different and beautiful on its own!

Happy Day
Multi-Layer Petals

This time I used my layered flower cut files with monochromatic patterned papers to create each layer. The additional step of distressing the edges of every single flower petal helps create contrast between all the layers, which might otherwise blend into one another a bit. I placed the flowers in rainbow order again and in a wreath configuration because wreaths always, always look beautiful!

You two had so much fun at the Cheyenne Mtn Zoo! We bought food sticks and you even caught a few of the birds. So fun!

APR 0 2 2022

THIS RIGHT HERE

CATCHING BUDGIES

HAND STITCHING

Hand stitching is one of my favorite techniques, but it's also the most time consuming. Layouts that feature hand stitching can take upward of 30 hours—but I love every single second. It's a great chance to multitask; try listening to a podcast or audiobook or watching a show while stitching. You can embroider patterns on papers. You can utilize cut files meant for stitching. You can stitch through die cuts and create stitched details on stickers, or even embroider through fabric and add it to a layout! No matter what you choose, I am sure you will love the results and hand-stitch on your pages whenever you have the time.

SUPPLIES

- Photos: (1) 2 ½" x 3", (1) 3" x 2½"
- White cardstock *(for page base)*
- Motif patterned paper
- Paper piercer
- Foam piercing mat
- Rainbow of embroidery threads
- Hand-stitching needle
- Rainbow-striped patterned paper
- Adhesive
- Letter stickers
- Sentiment sticker
- Journaling pen
- Roller date stamp
- Stamping ink

FINISHED SIZE: 12" SQUARE

STEP 1: Pierce stitching holes. Place a foam piercing mat behind your chosen motif paper, then use a paper piercer to make holes around the motifs that you want to embroider, leaving about ⅛" between each hole. Skip the right column of motifs.

STEP 2: Prepare the paper and threads. For the design, and to save yourself stitching time, you want to leave room for photos at the end. Tear off the right column of unpierced motifs. Then choose coordinating colors of embroidery floss and get ready for a stitch fest! (If you need any help achieving the specific stitches, there are plenty of tutorials on YouTube.)

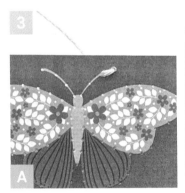
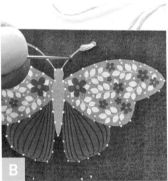
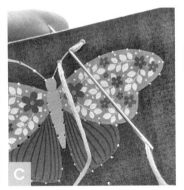

STEP 3: Stitch the antennae and body. For the antennae and body, use backstitch.

BACKSTITCH

- Start with an arm's length of thread, thread the needle, and tie a knot at the end.

- At the end of one antenna, bring the needle up through the back and pull the thread through until the knot catches at the back.

- Pass the needle down through the next hole and pull until the thread is taut (not tight—otherwise, the paper may tear) (A).

- Bring the needle up through the next hole from the back to the front and pull the thread taut (B).

- Pass the needle back down through the previous hole (this is why it's called backstitch). Pull the thread through until it's taut (C).

- Bring the needle up through the next hole from the back to the front and pull the thread taut.

- Pass the needle back down through the previous hole and pull the thread through until it's taut.

- Repeat until the entire shape is stitched, then tie a knot on the back side and trim any excess thread (D).

 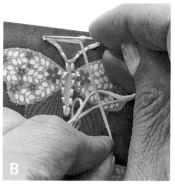  

STEP 4: Stitch the antennae ends. At the ends of each antenna, stitch a French knot.

FRENCH KNOT

- Start with an arm's length of thread, thread the needle, and tie a knot at the end.
- At the end of one antenna, bring the needle up through the back and pull the thread through until the knot catches at the back.
- Wrap the thread twice around the needle (A).
- Pass the needle back down through the same

hole, being careful not to get caught up in the knot you made previously (B).

- Pull the thread until it's taut. The wrapped thread will create a knot (C).
- Bring the needle up through the next hole where you want to make a French knot and repeat (D).
- When you're finished making French knots, tie the thread off and trim any excess.

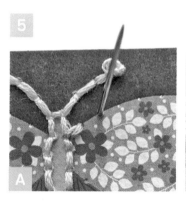 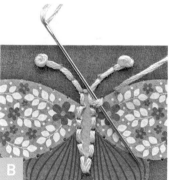 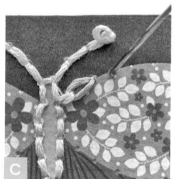 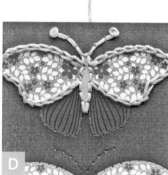

STEP 5: Stitch the top wings. For the top wings, use chain stitch.

CHAIN STITCH

- Start with an arm's length of thread, thread the needle, and tie a knot at the end.
- Choose a hole at one end of a wing to start. Bring the needle up through the back and pull the thread through until the knot catches at the back.
- Pass the needle down through the next hole and pull until the thread is taut.
- Go back up through the previous hole and down the same next hole so you've stitched the same holes twice.
- Go up through the next empty hole and pull the thread taut (A).
- Pass the needle under the previous pair of

stitches to link them together (this is why it's called chain stitch) and pull the thread taut (B).

- Pass the needle down through the same hole you came up through before linking. You can see the finished single chain link.
- Bring the needle up through the next empty hole and pull the thread taut (C).
- Pass the needle under the previous stitches to link them together and pull the thread taut.
- Repeat until the entire shape is stitched, then tie a knot on the back side and trim any excess thread (D).

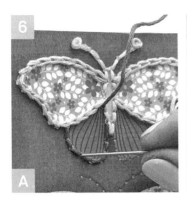

STEP 6: Stitch the bottom wings. For the bottom wings, do a bit of string art, which isn't an official stitch—I just "winged" it, if you will!

STRING ART

- Backstitch around the wings, following the backstitch steps explained previously.

- Once the edge of one bottom wing is stitched, bring the needle out through the top corner of the wing where it intersects with the body and top wing.

- Pass the needle down through one of the previously backstitched holes and pull the thread taut (A).

- Bring the needle up through the next hole over and go back down into the hole at the top (B).

- Bring the needle out the next hole along the bottom wing edge and go back down into the hole at the top.

- Repeat, making lines of thread until all the backstitched holes have been threaded (C).

- Stitch the other wing in the same way.

- Tie a knot at the back, then trim any excess (D).

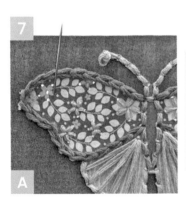
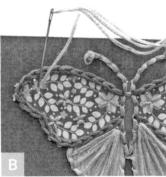

STEP 7: Stitch the top wings. Inside the top wings, stitch small flowers using a variation of fern stitch.

FERN STITCH (VARIATION)

- Pierce a hole at the end of all five flower petals as well as a hole in the flower center.

- Thread the needle with an arm's length of thread and tie a knot at the end.

- Bring the needle up through one petal end from the back to the front, pulling the thread until the knot catches at the back (A).

- Pass the needle down through the center hole

and pull it taut (B).

- Bring the needle up through the next petal end hole and then pass it down through the center hole again, pulling the thread taut (C).

- Repeat until all five petals of the flower are stitched, then move on to the next flower.

- Once all the flowers are stitched, tie a knot at the back and trim the excess thread (D).

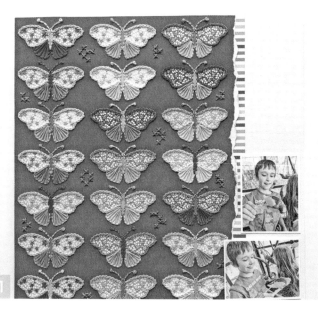

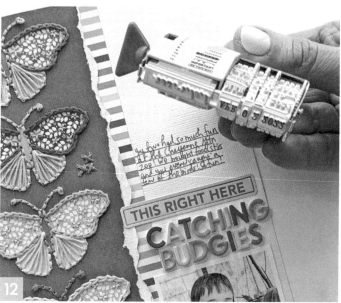

STEP 8: **Finish embroidering the butterflies.** Keep working hard until you've finished all the butterflies. It took me about an hour to stitch each butterfly, and there are 21 butterflies—you do the math! The back side is always a hot mess, but the front is a beautiful work of art.

STEP 9: **Add cross-stitching.** Add some cross-stitches to the background between the butterflies using thread of the same color as the background to visually break up that space and fill it with more texture.

STEP 10: **Cut a decorative strip.** Trim a 1 ½" x 12" piece of rainbow-striped paper and grab a sheet of textured white cardstock.

STEP 11: **Place the papers and photos.** Adhere the embroidered paper to the left side of the cardstock and tuck the striped paper under the torn right edge so it's just peeking out. Place two photos on the bottom right corner.

STEP 12: **Add the title, details, and journaling.** Create a title with mini alphabet stickers above the photos. Add a sentiment sticker above the title, then write journaling above that with a pen. Finally, stamp the date below the journaling.

Document This

Stitched Strips

Look for patterned papers that have stitching lines already printed on them—they make for the perfect place to add hand stitching! For this layout, I pierced holes through all the printed stitched lines and then did various stitches with a rainbow of thread colors to embroider a triangular piece of the paper. To balance out the busy stitching, I left the other half of the white cardstock background empty and tucked a bunch of floral die cuts under the edge of the stitched paper.

You Are Such a Lovely Girl

Connect-the-Dots Butterfly

I design many cut files specifically for hand stitching, such as this butterfly! First, the electronic cutting machine draws the design with a pencil onto my chosen paper or cardstock (this is a tool option on some machines), then it cuts the holes for stitching. Having the machine draw the design helps you see exactly where to stitch next—otherwise it just seems like a jumble of dots. I used a variegated pink/green/cream thread to backstitch through the butterfly and then cut the entire image out to use as a large focal element on my page.

Car Nap

Stitched Tiles

This tiles paper was just begging to be embroidered, so that's exactly what I did! Every design element printed on the paper is stitched with a chain stitch, French knot, or backstitch, so it's super soft to the touch. I did leave one square unstitched to not only save myself some time but also as a place to add a photo. Minimal embellishments around the photo ensure none of the stitching effort goes to waste.

One Fine Day

Pastel Stitched Motifs

This might be my favorite scrapbook layout ever! It's something about the soft colors, flowers, and, of course, the cute subject matter. I chose same-colored threads to do the stitching and made French knots, backstitches, and chain stitches. Between the sections of embroidered paper, I used a similar flower garden stencil with white modeling paste to add a subtle texture. Photos tucked into the bottom section of stitched paper and a title made with floral alphabet stickers along the torn edge complete this layout.

think happy thoughts

SHINE

SO HAPPY

FRIENDS FOREVER

12/12/21

You and Amy are just the cutest!
Snuggling on Rachel's old chair in my
happy scrappy place. Melts my heart!

STARS

Repetition is my most common technique when scrapping, and one easy way to create repetition is to use a single shape over and over. Whether the shape is hearts, butterflies, circles, triangles, or, as in this case, stars, a single shape repeated with lots of patterned papers creates a stunning effect. Punches, cut files, stamps, and stickers make creating multiples of the same shape a breeze. I often place the repeated shape in a wreath or frame around a singular photo. Let me show you how to use stars to elevate your scrapbooking!

SUPPLIES

- Photo: (1) 3" x 4"
- Yellow cardstock *(for page base)*
- Patterned papers
- Star punches (2 ³/₈", 1 ¹/₂", and ⁵/₈")
- Scoring board and tool
- White acrylic paint
- Paintbrush
- Watercolors
- Liquid adhesive
- Stickers
- Journaling pen
- Typed/printed journaling

FINISHED SIZE: 12" SQUARE

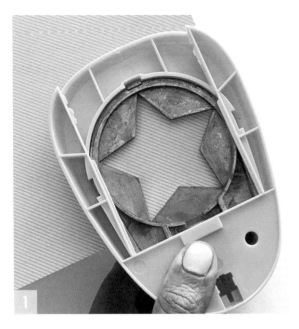

STEP 1: **Punch a star.** Punch a 2 ³⁄₈" star from patterned paper or cardstock.

STEP 2: **Score the first line.** Use a scoring board and tool to score straight down from one point of the star through the whole shape.

STEP 3: **Score the second line.** Rotate the star so the next point is at the top and score straight down again.

STEP 4: **Score the remaining lines.** Repeat to score from all the remaining points straight down until you've scored from all five points.

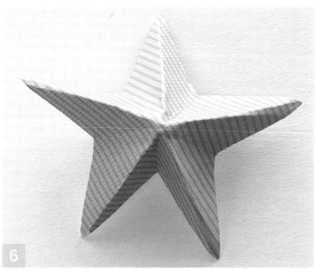

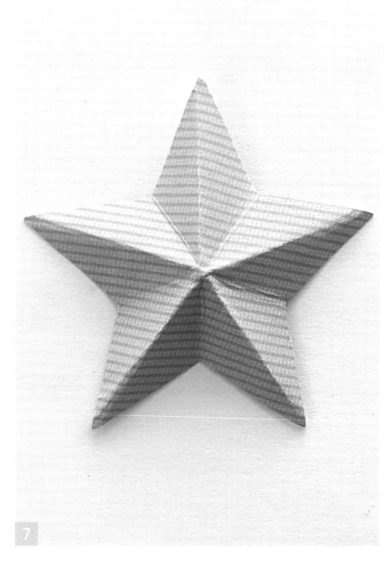

STEP 5: Pinch the lines. Pinch along the scored crease from one point to the center of the star, one section at a time, for all five points.

STEP 6: Finishing creasing all the lines. You'll end up with something like this. Keep pinching it and even folding it in half and partially opening it up again to really enhance the creases.

STEP 7: Open up the finished star. Press and crease the star one last time, then open it back up to see the finished three-dimensional shape.

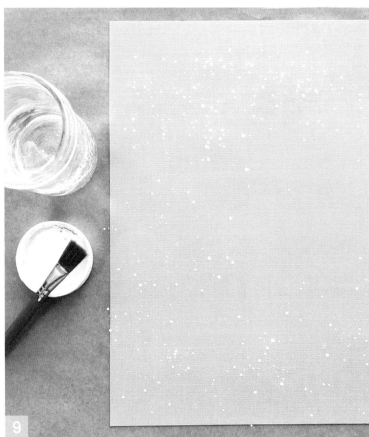

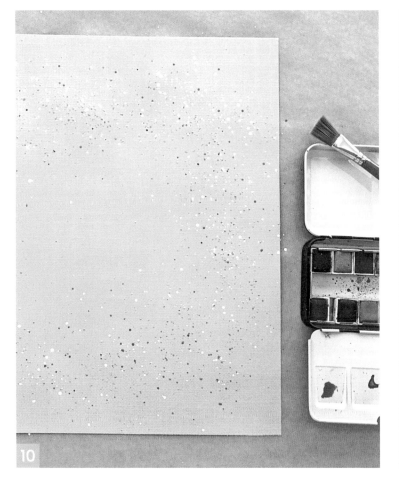

STEP 8: Create the rest of the stars. Punch, score, and crease sixteen 2 $\frac{3}{8}$" stars total and nineteen 1 $\frac{1}{2}$" stars total from a rainbow of patterned paper. Or make as many or as few from any size of star you'd like! Changing things up is a great way to make the design your own.

STEP 9: Splatter white paint on the background. On a piece of solid yellow cardstock or patterned paper, splash watered-down white acrylic paint to create a layer of interest. You can splatter the whole sheet or focus on the four sides.

STEP 10: Splatter rainbow watercolors. Once the acrylic paint dries, come in with a rainbow of watercolors to splatter more interesting layers on the background. All the paint colors will tie in with the colorful paper stars.

STEP 11: Add the photo and stars. Add a photo in the center, then frame the photo with the stars. Once you like the placement of the stars, place glue on the bottom sides of each star and press in place. Try not to flatten the stars too much as you're gluing them to ensure they retain their dimension.

STEP 12: Add miniature paper stars. Punch fourteen $\frac{5}{8}$" stars from a rainbow of patterned papers. I didn't score these—they are too tiny for my hands—but you could always give it a whirl! Adhere these tiny stars in the gaps between the larger stars.

STEP 13: Add sentiments and the date. Layer sentiment stickers over the top right side of the photo and tuck another sentiment under the top edge. Write the date with a journaling pen on a label sticker.

STEP 14: Add journaling. Type and print out some journaling, cut the words out, trim them into strips, and adhere them on the bottom left corner of the photo. I used the font Remington Noiseless, which resembles a vintage typewriter font, at size 8.

Brightside

Hand-Stitched Stars

It's no secret: I love hand stitching, and this page is no exception! I used one of my cut files to have an electronic cutting machine draw a frame of stars and then made holes for stitching on a painterly piece of patterned paper. I used thread colors to match the color underneath—for example, red thread on the red areas. It's an extra step, but look how lovely the tone-on-tone texture is! As with so many of my frame-style and stitching layouts, I don't want to cover up too much of it, so I placed a photo cluster in the center with all of the pertinent information like the title, date, and journaling.

Handsome Smile

Selective Star Backing

Here is a page that began with a stars background cut file. I used an electronic cutting machine to cut out the thin frame shape from dark blue paper, and then I backed only a few of the stars with patterned papers. I backed the largest star with a photo. Sometimes, less is more—even for this "more is more" gal.

You Are Awesome

Origami Star Wreath

This page was extra fun to make! I made 12 origami stars from a rainbow of patterned papers, placed them in a wreath design, and stitched over them several times to keep them in place permanently. YouTube and books are great resources for learning simple origami techniques that pair perfectly with patterned papers and scrapbooking.

All-Star Kiddo

Layers of Multimedia Stars

More star punches for the win! First, I used a star confetti stencil and scraped modeling paste through it to create a layer on a colorful polka-dot paper background. Once that was dry, I painted sections of watercolors on top. Then I punched a whole bunch of different-sized stars from patterned papers and took the time to distress all the edges. I clustered the stars in color groups across the background and adhered them in place with foam squares. It was lots of steps and layers, but I love the result!

CARDS

Handmade cards are all the rage right now! They are a great form of creativity and expression. All the techniques that you use to create scrapbook pages can be applied to the front of a card. With its more limited real estate, a card can often take a lot less time than a complete layout, and the reward to the recipient is more than worth it.

CONGRATULATIONS

We all deserve a little congratulations now and again! Whether it's a pay raise, new job, new home, new baby, or another significant celebration, it's always fun to receive that bit of recognition with a thoughtful handmade card. Using triangle punches makes creating the banner effect on this project very easy, but you can also cut out individual triangles without too much extra effort. And the stitching really makes the banner look real!

SUPPLIES

- Cardstock
- Patterned papers
- Two sizes of triangle punches (1 ½" and 2")
- Stencil
- Modeling paste
- Spatula

- Liquid adhesive
- Adhesive (*strong tape or a lightweight adhesive*)
- Sewing machine
- White thread
- Alphabet stickers
- Sentiment sticker

FINISHED SIZE: 5 ½" WIDE x 4 ¼" HIGH

STEP 1: Make the card base. Trim textured cardstock to 5 1/2" x 8 1/2" and fold it in half vertically to create the card base.

STEP 2: Punch small triangles. Choose nine solid colors of patterned paper, one patterned paper with at least nine different colors, or nine colors of cardstock. Punch a 1" (base) x 1 1/8" (height) triangle from all nine colors.

STEP 3: Punch large triangles. Punch a bigger 1 1/4" (base) x 1 1/2" (height) triangle from the same nine colors.

STEP 4: Apply the stencil. Place a piece of scrap paper behind your card and grab a stencil, modeling paste, and spatula. Set the stencil over the front of the card. Gently and evenly scrape the modeling paste through it.

STEP 5: Remove the stencil. Carefully lift the stencil off to reveal the fun pattern.

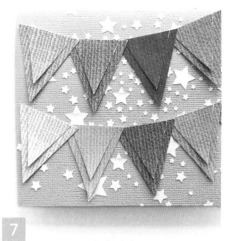

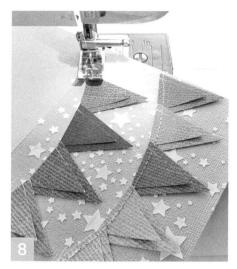

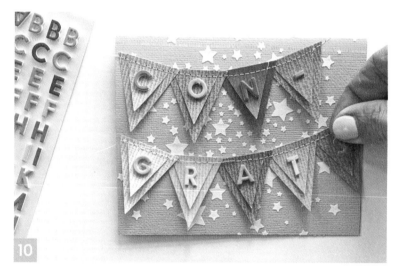

STEP 6: Glue the pennants together. While the modeling paste is drying, layer the matched pairs of triangles together with the top, straight edges aligned. Adhere them together across the top with a thin line of liquid adhesive.

STEP 7: Arrange the pennants. Place the pennants in two rows (four along the top, five along the bottom) across the front of the card. Adhere them using strong tape if you're not going to add machine stitching, or light adhesive if you do plan to add machine stitching.

STEP 8: Stitch the pennants. Use white thread and a basic running stitch to machine-stitch across the tops of the two banners.

STEP 9: Bend the pennants. Gently bend up (without creasing) the bottoms of all the individual pennant layers to create dimension.

STEP 10: Add the message. Place "CON-GRATS" letters tone on tone on the pennants to spell out the sentiment.

STEP 11: Add additional embellishment. Attach a secondary sentiment sticker at the top to finish the card.

my deepest sympathies

SYMPATHY

Not every day is sunshine and roses, that's for sure. So when someone is down on their luck, sick, recovering from surgery, or going through a tough loss, a little pick-me-up in the form of happy mail is sure to brighten their day. The message on the front of the card is easy to customize to suit your reason for sending the card—you may consider changing "my deepest sympathies" to "get well soon," "thinking of you," "you'll pull through," or "I'm here for you."

SUPPLIES

- Patterned papers
- Rolled flowers digital cut file
- Electronic cutting machine
- Liquid adhesive
- Heart digital cut file
- White cardstock
- Typed/printed sentiment

FINISHED SIZE: 4 ½" SQUARE

STEP 1: Prepare the rolled flowers. Die-cut about 30 to 35 rolled flower cut files that are 2" across from colorful patterned papers.

STEP 2: Start rolling. Grab one rolled flower with the pattern you want showing facing up. Starting at the outer end, begin rolling it up, toward you.

STEP 3: Continue rolling. Continue rolling the flower until you get almost all the way to the other end; you will see it grow in size (pictured is about halfway through). If you want a fuller flower, you can gently and carefully release the rolls until the flower is the size you want it. I kept mine rather tightly rolled.

STEP 4: Glue the flower. Dab liquid adhesive on the last little bit of the rolled flower and press the rolled portion into it until the glue sets.

STEP 5: Finish the flower. Bend the petals outward or press the edges flatter to create more dimension and a more lifelike flower.

STEP 6: Make the rest of the flowers. Repeat for all the rolled flowers until you have as many finished flowers as you need. Fair warning: these can be addicting to make!

STEP 7: Start building the heart. Die-cut a 4" x 3 ½" heart cut file from smooth white cardstock. Add a dab of glue to the center of the heart and place the first flower.

STEP 8: Finishing building the heart. Continue gluing flowers around the first one until the entire heart is covered.

STEP 9: Attach the heart to the card. Trim a piece of patterned paper to 9" x 4 ½" and fold it in half horizontally to create the card base. Glue the heart to the card base.

STEP 10: Add a sentiment. Type, print out, and trim a sentiment on white paper, notching the ends to turn it a little banner shape. I used the font Remington Noiseless, which resembles a vintage typewriter font, at size 8. Glue the sentiment across the front of the card to finish it.

BIRTHDAY

Every person I know has a birthday at some point in the year—so why not wish them a happy special day with a cute and colorful card? There are so many possibilities for customizing this design. Instead of a rainbow of backing colors for the sentiment, why not go with a more limited palette of the recipient's favorite colors? You could also choose stickers specific to their tastes, so dig through your stash—maybe you have cute cat, flower, emoji, or other special stickers that will make them smile.

SUPPLIES

- White cardstock
- "HAPPY BIRTHDAY TO YOU" digital cut file
- Electronic cutting machine
- Patterned papers

- Pencil
- Liquid adhesive
- Banner die cut
- Heart enamel shapes

FINISHED SIZE: 5 ½" WIDE x 4" HIGH

STEP 1: Prepare the sentiment. Die-cut the "HAPPY BIRTHDAY TO YOU" cut file at 4 ⅞" across from textured white cardstock.

STEP 2: Choose letter colors. Select 18 patterned papers to back each of the 18 letters and decide in which order you want them to appear. Since these letters are very small, this is a great opportunity to use leftover paper scraps.

STEP 3: Trace the first letter. Flip both the cut file and the chosen patterned paper over to the back side, slide the patterned paper underneath the letter you want to trace, and then trace inside the letter shape with a pencil.

STEP 4: Trace and cut out all the letters. Cut out the letter about ⅛" larger all around than your pencil lines. If you cut it out exactly on the lines, the letter will fall right through the cut file. Repeat the tracing and cutting process for all 18 letters.

STEP 5: Start gluing the letters. Add liquid adhesive onto the back of two or three letters of the sentiment at a time, then place the patterned letters in their coordinating spots.

STEP 6: Finish gluing the letters. Once all of the letters are in place, flip it over and say, "Ta da!" It's always such a fun reveal moment when you get to see the result of your hard work.

STEP 7: Prepare the card base. Trim a piece of patterned paper or cardstock to 5 ½" x 8" and fold it in half vertically to create the card base.

STEP 8: Attach the sentiment. Place foam squares on the back of the sentiment and attach it to the upper portion of the card front.

STEP 9: Add a banner. Attach a colorful banner die cut below the sentiment, trim the excess off the sides, and bend up the individual pennants to add dimension.

STEP 10: Add stickers. To finish, adhere heart enamel stickers tone on tone to five of the letters.

THANK YOU

Thank-you cards are the ones I make and send most often. My grandma Cathie Taylor always taught me it's polite to say thanks with a traditional snail-mail card, so every time we get a gift, whether big or small, we're sure to send a note of thanks. When the person you're thanking receives this gem, they'll be delighted by the quirky button touches and the careful composition you created for them. Enjoy rummaging through your button collection to find a grouping that tickles your fancy!

SUPPLIES

- Patterned papers
- Buttons
- Liquid adhesive
- Label sticker
- Letter stickers
- Sewing machine *(optional)*
- White thread *(optional)*

FINISHED SIZE: 5 ½" WIDE x 4 ¼" HIGH

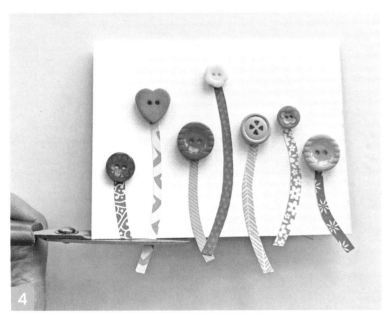
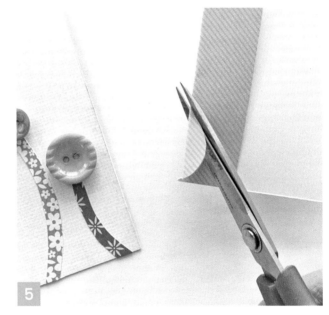

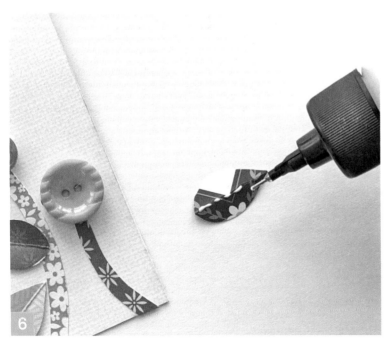

STEP 1: Prepare the card base. Trim a piece of patterned paper to 5 ½" x 8 ½" and fold it in half vertically to create the card base.

STEP 2: Add buttons. Attach seven buttons in rainbow order and staggered across the front of the card.

STEP 3: Cut stems. Hand-cut seven curved stems from green and blue patterned papers. Tuck one under each of the buttons.

STEP 4: Finish the stems. Secure the stems in place with liquid adhesive, then trim any excess paper hanging over the card edge.

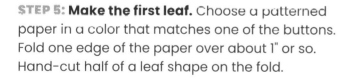

STEP 5: Make the first leaf. Choose a patterned paper in a color that matches one of the buttons. Fold one edge of the paper over about 1" or so. Hand-cut half of a leaf shape on the fold.

STEP 6: Make the rest of the leaves. Use the first leaf as a template to trace and cut out a leaf from six more patterned papers, matching each paper to one of the buttons. Add a line of glue to the back spine of each leaf and attach them to the stems.

STEP 7: Bend the leaves. Holding the leaves down carefully so that they stay adhered, fold up the edges of the leaves to add dimension.

STEP 8: Add a label. Place a label sticker on the bottom right corner of the card.

STEP 9: Add a sentiment. Add "THANK YOU" letter stickers in a rainbow of colors on top of the label sticker.

STEP 10: Add stitching. With white thread, machine-stitch using a basic running stitch twice horizontally on top of the sentiment. Trim any excess thread.

ANNIVERSARY

Let someone know how special they are and how much you love them, and wish them a happy anniversary with a beautiful card that you've made with tender love and care! This design also works like a charm for Valentine's Day. Your choice of decorative papers is a focus for this project—have fun punching and pairing up cohesive or contrasting stacks of hearts. The stitching is optional, but I highly recommend it for this project because it will make the card super durable and doesn't take long to execute.

SUPPLIES

- Patterned papers
- Three sizes of heart punches
- Adhesive
- Cardstock
- Sewing machine (*optional*)

- White thread (*optional*)
- Typed/printed sentiment
- Foam squares
- White acrylic paint
- Paintbrush
- Enamel dots

FINISHED SIZE: 4 ¼" WIDE x 5 ½" HIGH

STEP 1: Punch the hearts. Punch three concentric sizes of hearts from a piece of patterned paper. I used 1", ½", and ¼" heart punches.

STEP 2: Stack the hearts. Each card requires 15 sets of hearts. I punched 30 sets of concentric hearts to make two cards. Arrange the hearts into piles of the same pattern.

STEP 3: Adhere the heart stacks. If you are not going to use a sewing machine to attach the hearts to the cards, use a strong adhesive to attach the layers of hearts together. If you do plan to use a sewing machine, use just a little bit of a temporary adhesive to attach the layers together. The less glue you use, the less the needle will gum up.

STEP 4: Select your arrangement. Once each separate heart stack is adhered together, figure out the order in which you'd like them to appear on the card—whether that's in rainbow order, a random colorway, or a curated collection of colors.

STEP 5: Prep the card bases. Trim two pieces of cardstock to 5 ½" x 8 ½". Fold each piece in half horizontally to create a card base. Complete all the following steps for each card to make two cards.

STEP 6: Add the center heart. Find the center of the front of the card (at 2 ⅛" from the spine and 2 ¾" from the top) and attach the first heart stack there. Again, use a light touch of temporary glue if you're adding machine stitching, or strong permanent adhesive if you're not.

STEP 7: Add the other hearts. Attach the rest of the heart stacks in a grid design to the card front, leaving about an ⅛" gap between each one.

STEP 8: Sew the hearts. Use white thread and a basic running stitch to stitch down the center of the three rows of hearts. Trim any excess thread.

STEP 9: Add dimension. Pinch and bend the edges of all the hearts upward to create texture and dimension.

STEP 10: Add a message. Type, print out, and trim a sentiment for the front of the card. I used the font Remington Noiseless, which resembles a vintage typewriter font, at size 8. Attach the sentiment with foam squares near the bottom of the card.

STEP 11: Splatter with paint. Splash watered-down white acrylic paint across the front of the card to create cohesion and add another layer of interest.

STEP 12: Add dots. Scatter enamel dots in shades that match the card base color between and around the hearts.

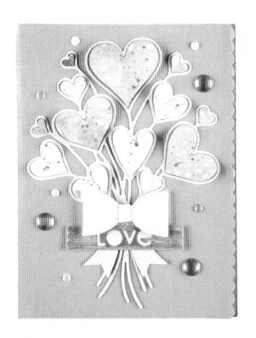

Love

Heart Bouquet

FINISHED SIZE: 4 ¼" WIDE x 5 ½" HIGH

SUPPLIES: cardstock, watercolors, white acrylic paint, gold paint, paintbrush, enamel dots, heart bouquet metal die, manual die cut machine, sentiment, paper bow, deco scissors, adhesive

Die-cut the bouquet from white cardstock, then paint the normally discarded inner pieces and place them back inside the hearts. Embellish with enamel dots scattered across the background for pops of color and interest. Use deco scissors on the card edge for a fun-to-touch detail.

Love

Quilt-Inspired Heart

FINISHED SIZE: 5" SQUARE

SUPPLIES: patterned papers, 1" square punch, puffy dot stickers, wood veneer heart, sentiment die cut, tab die cut, adhesive

Punch 1" squares from patterned papers, cut the squares in half diagonally to make triangles, then piece the triangles together in a quilt-inspired heart shape to create a standout design on your card. Add puffy dot stickers tone on tone for little bits of eye candy.

Thanks

Hand-Stitched Rainbow

FINISHED SIZE: 4 ¼" WIDE x 5 ½" HIGH

SUPPLIES: cardstock, patterned papers, white embroidery floss, hand-sewing needle, "THANKS" digital cut file, electronic cutting machine, adhesive

Add hand-stitched details to the "THANKS" cut file to create texture. Use colorful papers to back the sentiment and for the card base to create an eye-catching design.

Thanks a Bunch

Doily Background

FINISHED SIZE: 5 ½" SQUARE

SUPPLIES: cardstock, patterned paper, chipboard stickers, flower paper clip, floral and leaf die cuts, doily digital cut file, electronic cutting machine, typed/printed sentiment, adhesive

Back an intricate doily cut file with a single colorful patterned paper, then cluster embellishments in the center to make a quick and easy card.

Smile

Butterflies and Splatter Background

FINISHED SIZE: 4 ¼" WIDE x 5 ½" HIGH

SUPPLIES: cardstock, patterned paper, white acrylic paint, watercolors, paintbrush, acrylic sentiment, adhesive

Add pops of color to a plain white cardstock base with watercolors and white acrylic paint. Fussy-cut butterflies from a piece of patterned paper and attach them at their centers only so the wings can bend and lift off the background.

Thank You Very Much

Pink Floral

FINISHED SIZE: 5 ½" WIDE x 4 ¼" HIGH

SUPPLIES: patterned papers, floral and leaf die cuts, typed/printed sentiment, white thread, bend-up flower digital cut file, electronic cutting machine, adhesive

Bend up the petals of a bend-up flower cut file to create fun dimension on a card base. Tangle up some thread and place it under the sentiment and die cuts to add some whimsy!

MINI ALBUMS

Surely you've been there—you just came home from a great trip, wedding, or other event and want to immortalize it, but you have so many photos and memories you want to include that you think it'll take pages and pages (and hours and hours) to capture! Well, a mini album is the perfect solution: you can creatively pack a ton of content into bite-sized pages in a bound collection that becomes a true handheld memory. Let me show you how!

To see all of the finished pages of all three albums and get even more inspired, check out my video flip-throughs here:

bit.ly/paigeevansmakeyourmemory

ELASTIC BINDING

I just celebrated 15 years of marriage to my husband, so I thought it would be fun to find a photo from every year so far, see how we've changed, and fondly remember all our adventures throughout this decade and a half! This album includes 32 interior pages, so there is plenty of room to pack in the memories.

SUPPLIES

- Photos: (15) 1 ³/₄" square
- Patterned papers
- Scoring board and tool
- Patterned transparency
- Corner rounder
- Liquid adhesive
- Charms

- Buttons
- Heart paper clips
- Elastic cording
- Temporary adhesive
- Stickers
- Die cuts
- Other embellishments
- Journaling pen
- Foam squares

FINISHED SIZE: 3 ¼" WIDE x 3 ½" HIGH x 1" THICK

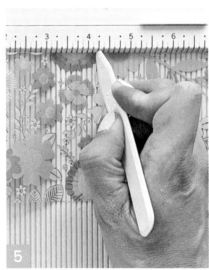

STEP 1: Cut the base pages. Cut a blocked paper in half, then trim those halves into 3" x 6" blocks. A blocked paper makes this first step easy, but if you don't have a similar blocked paper, trim cardstock or patterned papers into eight 3" x 6" sections.

STEP 2: Score the base pages. Score each 3" x 6" block at 3", between the two sections, and fold the block in half to crease the score line.

STEP 3: Pair the base pages. Stack the eight folded blocks together in sets of two to create four sets.

STEP 4: Cut the cover. Trim a piece of patterned transparency to 3 ½" x 12", then score it at 3 ¼" from the left edge. Fold the scored line over.

STEP 5: Shape the spine. Open the transparency back up, then score it at 4 ¼". Fold this scored line over the same way you did the first. The two folds together create a 1" spine for the mini album. Increase or decrease your second score placement to widen or narrow the spine as desired.

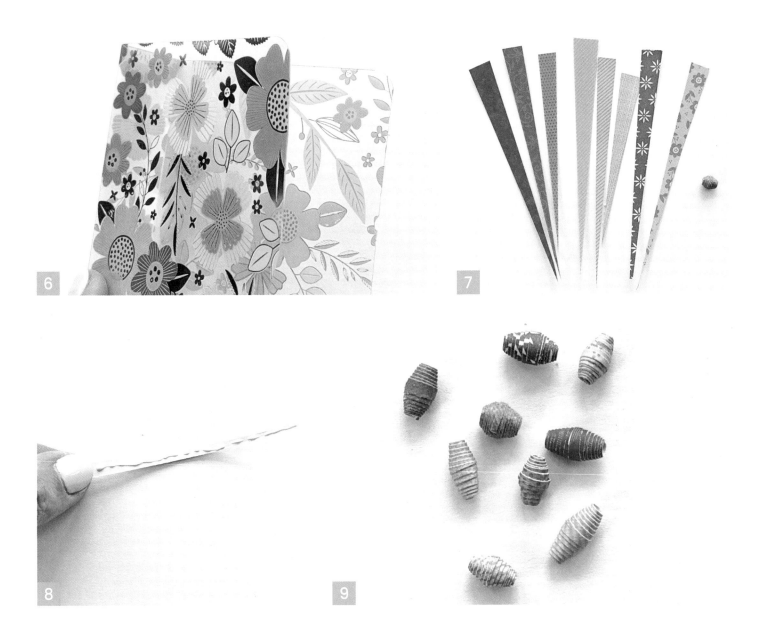

STEP 6: Round the cover corners. Trim the transparency to 7 $\frac{1}{2}$" long, then round the corners (they are typically rather sharp). You can use a $\frac{1}{2}$" corner rounder or simply a pair of scissors.

STEP 7: Prepare wedges for paper beads. Let's make some paper beads! This is another one of those techniques where once you make one, you won't be able to stop! From different patterned papers, trim thin, pointed wedges about $\frac{1}{4}$" wide at the widest point and 5" long.

STEP 8: Roll the beads. Starting at the widest point, begin rolling up each wedge of paper. When there is about 3" left to roll, add liquid adhesive to the back side of the paper, then finish rolling it up. Hold the end in place until the glue sets. You have a paper bead!

STEP 9: Finish the beads. Make as many or as few beads as you'd like. I created nine for this mini album from a rainbow of mostly solid-patterned papers.

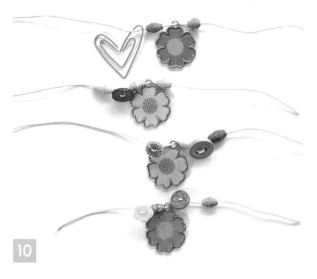

10

11

12

13

14

STEP 10: Prepare the elastic binding. Choose an assortment of other embellishments to dangle from the spine, such as charms, buttons, and paper clips. Trim four pieces of elastic cording to about 7" each, then string on the paper beads and embellishments as desired, centered in the middle of each piece of elastic.

STEP 11: Tie on the binding. Tie the first piece of elastic around the spine of the mini album (with the embellishments on the outside) as tight as you can in a double knot. Continue with the remaining three pieces of elastic cording. To help keep the cords in place, you can cut four very tiny slits at the top and bottom edges of the spine and wedge the cords into them.

STEP 12: Insert the base pages. Slide the sets of stacked pages under the elastic cording, centered in the creased middle, to complete the mini album base. It's time for photos and embellishing! But first, trim the excess elastic cording ends close to the knots.

STEP 13: Decide on photo placement. It is easier to work on the pages if they are not bound into the cover, so remove them and figure out where you want to add photos. Attach the photos in place with temporary adhesive.

STEP 14: Embellish the front cover. Decorate the cover however you'd like. I added a flower that was left over from one of my previous scrapbooking projects. For the title, I layered a label die cut onto a label sticker and created the title with a mix of alphabet stickers, sentiment stickers, and an epoxy ampersand sticker.

STEP 15: Embellish the pages. Decorate the photo pages one by one. Once you like everything you've added, use permanent glue to attach everything in place. I included various number stickers with every photo to indicate the year it was taken, from 2008 to 2022. Don't forget to add personal notes!

STEP 16: Finish embellishing. For a final decorative touch, from another piece of the same patterned paper I used to make the foundation pages, I fussy-cut all of the same flowers and attached them in place with foam squares for added dimension on those pages. If you don't have the same paper, you could add floral die cuts or even more photos to those pages.

ADDITIONAL IDEAS

- Need more pages? It's easy to add eight more pages by simply adding two more 3" x 6" blocks to the mix.

- Increase the overall size of the album by trimming larger papers and a larger transparency cover.

STANDOUT SHAPE

Mini albums that are built from a single interesting shape are probably my favorite to make because there are so many options—so many shapes exist in this world! As I worked on this book, it was springtime, my favorite season, so I decided to dedicate this album to spring 2022! I began how I usually begin with shaped mini albums: designing a digital cut file. Every butterfly is a slightly different shape and size, which makes turning every page a fun experience. This album includes 16 pages (including the front and back "covers").

SUPPLIES

- Photos:
  (9) 2" square, (1)
  3" x 2", (3) 2" x 3"
- Cardstock
- Patterned papers
- Butterflies digital
  cut file
- Electronic cutting
  machine
- Stencils

- Modeling paste
- Spatula
- Sewing needle
- Embroidery threads
- Temporary adhesive
- Stickers
- Die cuts
- Enamel dots
- Heart paper clips

- Journaling pens
- Typed/printed words
  and sentiments
- Standard 1/4" hole
  punch
- Hole reinforcer punch
- Liquid adhesive
- Loose-leaf 1"
  binder ring

FINISHED SIZE: APPROXIMATELY 6" WIDE x 5" HIGH x 1 1/2" THICK

STEP 1: Prep the cover page. Die-cut an intricate lattice cover butterfly cut file from white cardstock and back it with a rainbow of patterned papers. Cut a solid butterfly cut file and attach it onto the back to make the back side clean and easier to embellish later.

STEP 2: Cut the other pages. Die-cut seven more butterfly cut files from a rainbow of patterned papers or cardstock. They don't all have to be the same shape, but they should be close in size to the cover butterfly.

STEP 3: Stencil some pages. Take this opportunity to experiment with mixed media on these small pages! Grab a stencil, some modeling paste, and a spatula. Place the stencil over a page, gently scrape the paste through, and then lift off the stencil to reveal the gorgeousness. Add mixed media to as many pages as you like; I stenciled two of them.

STEP 4: Prep for stitching. I always love to include a stitching option with my mini album cut files so that I can add hand-stitched details. Choose coordinating colors of embroidery floss and spend some time hand-stitching around the border holes of each butterfly page.

STEP 5: Finish stitching. I used running stitch, chain stitch, whipstitch, and backstitch on various pages. I just love the texture and homespun look and feel that stitching adds.

STEP 6: Place front photos. Set out all the pages and figure out the order you want them in, keeping the patterns of the fronts and backs in mind and how they look next to each other. I like to have a busy pattern paired with a more solid color and then repeat that throughout the pages. Use temporary adhesive to stick photos onto the fronts of the pages.

STEP 7: Place back photos. Then place more photos onto the backs of all the pages. For pages where a front photo visibly hangs off an edge, back it with the same size photo on the opposite side to cover that area up—this will neaten the overall look.

STEP 8: Begin embellishing. Find stickers, die cuts, and anything else you have that go along with your theme. Since my album is spring themed and the embellishment collection I used was full of flowers and bright colors, it was easy to find pieces that evoked feelings of spring. Focus on larger embellishments first and glue them in place along with the photos.

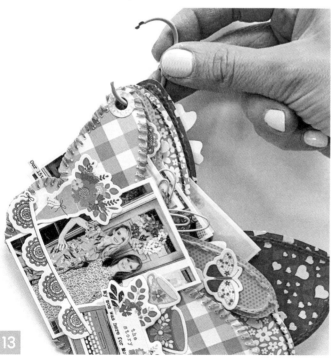

STEP 9: Embellish the backs. Flip the pages over to the back sides and repeat with more large, coordinating embellishments to help tell the story of your photos.

STEP 10: Add smaller details. Add medium and small embellishments to the pages. At this point in the process, I typically start working on the pages one by one instead of all at once. Add typed, printed, and trimmed journaling strips and handwritten journaling to help tell the story throughout the album.

STEP 11: Punch the holes. Once all the pages are finished, use a standard ¼" hole punch to punch a hole through the top left corner of the first page. Use the placement of that first hole as a template to punch a hole through the top left corner of the rest of the pages.

STEP 12: Add reinforcement. Use a hole reinforcer punch to make a little paper ring for the front and back of every punched hole. Add liquid adhesive to the reinforcers and adhere them in place. I love that the reinforcers not only reinforce but also add a pop of color to the pages, depending on the paper or cardstock that you punch them from.

STEP 13: Bind the pages. Attach all the pages together with a 1" loose-leaf binder ring. Slide the last page onto the ring first, followed by the second-to-last page, etc., until you add the cover. All that is left to do is to admire your beautiful work!

ADDITIONAL IDEAS

- Dangle charms and beads from the binder ring to create a fun and eclectic finishing touch.

- Change the shape of the base! Use hearts, flowers, circles, triangles, pennants, Christmas ornaments—if you can attach the pages together with a binder ring, you can make a mini album out of it!

ACCORDION

For my 15th wedding anniversary, my mom flew down from Seattle to watch the kids while my husband and I went on a weekend getaway just an hour south of home. This heart-shaped accordion-style mini album features photos from our trip and documents a little of our love story! This album includes 12 pages (including the front and back "covers").

SUPPLIES

- Photos: (11) 1 ³/₄" square
- Patterned papers
- Two hearts digital cut file
- Electronic cutting machine
- Sewing machine
- Rainbow of threads
- Scoring board and tool
- Liquid adhesive
- Temporary adhesive
- Stickers
- Die cuts
- Embellishments
- Journaling pens
- ¹/₈" hole punch
- Pom-pom tassel

FINISHED SIZE: 3 ³/₄" WIDE x 3 ¹/₂" HIGH CLOSED, 18 ³/₄" WIDE x 3 ¹/₂" HIGH OPEN; 1" THICK

STEP 1: Cut the album pages. Die-cut six 3 ³/₄" x 3 ½" heart cut files from patterned papers. (The two hearts in the digital cut file are slightly different sizes, so use either only the one with stitching dots or only the one without.) Figure out which patterns you want on the front and back and the order from left to right. Remember that when the accordion is fully extended, you will "read" it all in a row on the front side, and you'll flip it over to the back side to "read" the entire back.

STEP 2: Stitch the hearts. Machine-stitch with a running stitch and then a zigzag stitch around the border of each heart using a coordinating color of thread.

STEP 3: Score and crease the first heart. Double-check your heart order and start with the front side of the first heart—this will be your album "cover." Score a line at 3 ³/₈" from the left edge of this first heart. Crease that scored edge back and forth (in both directions).

STEP 4: Score and crease the second heart. On the second heart (still on the front side), score a line at ³/₈" from the left edge and at 3 ³/₈" from the left edge. Bend those scored edges back and forth.

5

STEP 5: Score and crease the remaining hearts. Repeat scoring and folding for the next three hearts. Then, for the last heart, score at ³/₈" from the left edge only, creasing that edge back and forth as usual.

STEP 6: Glue the first heart. Add glue to the tabs of the first and second hearts and pinch them together until the glue has set. Make sure the tabs are both facing up (to the top side).

6

STEP 7: Finish gluing. Glue the rest of the hearts together at the tabs to assemble the mini-album structure. All the tabs should be facing the same direction, so the back side (pictured here) is smooth and flat.

STEP 8: Trim threads. Trim the excess thread ends (or leave them long if you prefer a more ragged look!).

7

8

9

10

11

STEP 9: Decide photo placement. Figure out where you want photos. Use temporary glue to affix them in place as you work on the pages. Put photos on both the front and back sides.

STEP 10: Decorate the front cover. Create a title on the front of the first heart with a cluster of die cuts, stickers, handwritten words, enamel and puffy heart stickers, and more.

STEP 11: Decorate the remaining pages. Throughout the rest of the pages, add larger embellishments first, such as die cuts and stickers. Continue embellishing with medium and then small embellishments, like enamel dots and sentiment stickers. Complete the front side entirely, then flip the whole thing over and embellish the back side.

STEP 12: Punch a hole. Use a ⅛" hole punch to make a hole through the top left side of the front cover heart, just to the inside of the stitching line.

STEP 13: Add a tassel. String a pom-pom tassel charm through the hole, securing it with a lark's head knot.

STEP 14: Fold and store. Fold the album up accordion-style for storing. You could also keep it closed with a tied ribbon or a clip if it's not too thick.

12

13

ADDITIONAL IDEAS

- Die-cut larger hearts to increase the overall size of the mini album—that means you can add larger photos and even more embellishments!

- Add hand stitching instead of machine stitching around each heart.

- The sizes of these pages are perfect for experimenting with mixed media such as stencils and inks/sprays.

14

Luxembourg

Elastic Binding

FINISHED SIZE: 4" WIDE x 4" HIGH x 2 ¼" THICK

This elastic binding album is heart shaped, and the cover is made from chipboard covered with patterned papers. Since the spine is extra wide, I was able to fit seven strings of elastic cording. I love the tactile embellishments on the cording, which include charms, tassels, and lots of handmade paper beads, as well as acrylic beads. The heart-shaped pages were first cut on an electronic cutting machine using a cut file, and then, as always, I added machine stitching to the edges of the pages to create texture and interest. Instead of stacking pages two together as in the featured elastic binding project, these pages are singles, so I was able to add a lot of thick embellishments without the album becoming too chunky!

Hallstatt, Austria

Standout Shape

FINISHED SIZE: 4" WIDE x 7" HIGH x 1" THICK

Another butterfly-shaped mini album? Yes! I've made many, and they all look completely different from one another. By changing the colors, patterns, embellishments, and photos, you'll have a similar but unique mini album documenting your memories. For this mini album, I really played into experimenting with mixed media and added machine stitching, stenciling with modeling paste, paints splashed on top, and more.

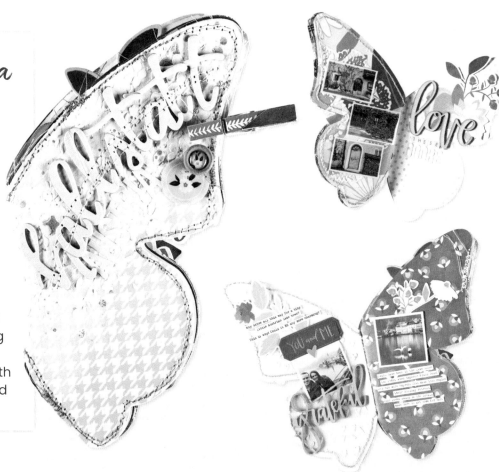

Here & Now

Accordion

FINISHED SIZE: 4" WIDE x 6" HIGH CLOSED; 1" THICK

This is one of the very first mini albums I taught how to create in my virtual classes! The front-side pages are all created vertically, then, when the album is flipped over to the back side, the pages switch to a horizontal orientation. The concept for assembling the base is essentially the same as in the featured accordion project: scoring tabs and attaching them in a row. Add your photos, then work on each page one at a time. Tie the album closed with a pair of stacked ribbons with charms dangling from the bow.

INDEX

Note: Page numbers in *italics* indicate projects and scrapbook layouts.

PULLOUT SCRAPBOOK PAPER

Are you ready to scrap?
The paper at the back of this book is designed
and perforated to be easily torn out and
used in your next scrapbooking project. These
designs are super-adaptable basics that
you'll surely find a use for.
Have fun making your memories!

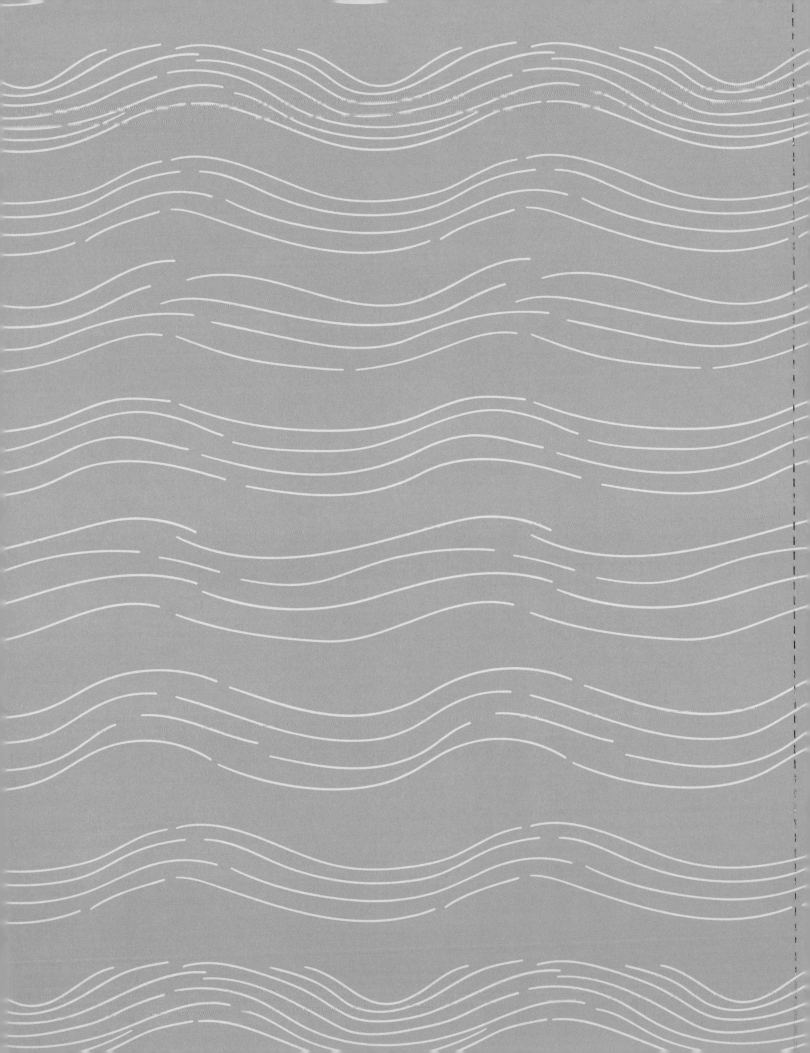